D0283762

THE
LOVE
TEST

THE
LOVE
TEST

Romance and Relationship Self-Quizzes

Developed by Psychologists and

Sociologists

VIRGINIA RUTTER, M.A., AND

PEPPER SCHWARTZ, PH.D.

A Perigee Book

A Perigee Book
Published by The Berkley Publishing Group
A member of Penguin Putnam Inc.
200 Madison Avenue
New York, NY 10016

First edition: February 1998

Published simultaneously in Canada.

The Putnam Berkley World Wide Web site address is
http://www.berkley.com

Library of Congress Cataloging-in-Publication Data

Rutter, Virginia Elisabeth
    The love test : romance and relationship self-quizzes developed by
    psychologists and sociologists / Virginia Rutter and Pepper Schwartz.
    —1st ed.
        p. cm.
    "A Perigee book."
    Includes bibliographical references.
    ISBN 0-399-52403-7
    1. Love.   2. Intimacy (Psychology)   3. Sex (Psychology)
    4. Marriage—Psychological aspects.   I. Schwartz, Pepper.
II.   Title.
BF575.L8R88   1998
158.2—dc21   97-33452
                                                         CIP

Printed in the United States of America
10   9   8   7   6   5   4   3

CONTENTS

SECTION 1

FALLING IN LOVE

What Kind of Lover Am I?

SECTION 2

STAYING IN LOVE AND BEING CLOSE

A Relationship Checkup

SECTION 3

KEY EMOTIONAL ISSUES

SECTION 4

SEX WITH SOMEONE YOU LOVE

SECTION 5

GETTING A FAIR DEAL

SECTION 6

SOME SERIOUS RELATIONSHIP ISSUES

Acknowledgments

The authors wish to thank all the sociologists, psychologists and psychotherapists who contributed their excellent work to this book. Drs. Shirley Glass, Susan and Clyde Hendrick, and Dana Crowley Jack were particularly generous with their thoughts and material. Other social scientists provided ideas to the authors, including Sara Berns, Neil Jacobson, and Stacey Prince.

The authors also had the benefit of feedback from a number of friends and colleagues who reviewed and discussed different sections of the book, including: Michael Heller, David Holiday, Ken and Tina Wagers, Ned and Joanna Fox, Adria Scharf, Matthew Hempleman, Emily and Jesse Jacobson, and Lorella Palazzo. In addition, Diane Sollee's optimism for couples' education (and her training of Virginia in writing for the public) was of great assistance to Virginia as she constructed this book.

Finally, the authors appreciate the support of the University of Washington Department of Sociology in their diverse creative endeavors. A special thanks to our friends at the U.W. Center for the Study of Demography and Ecology for their support.

THE
LOVE
TEST

INTRODUCTION

O ne of the fascinating things about studying sex and relationships (as we have been doing for many years) is that every topic is immediately relevant and very personal. This book will help you study your relationship and your love life using tests, questionnaires, and inventories from psychologists, sociologists, therapists, and other relationship experts.

Even though there are things that are common in nearly all relationships, it is still true that couples develop their own world and intimate space where the rules and experiences are intensely private and unique. Individuals who aren't in an intimate relationship at the present still think about how well their hopes and dreams will measure up to real life.

That intense kind of privacy is precious—and it even

helps inflame the passion and enrich the love. Our desire for love is so deep, private, and personal that we have trouble seeing ourselves objectively as a lover. We readily diagnose a friend's relationship or problems getting into one. But that's a romp in the park compared to getting perspective on our own behavior. We are too close to the subject of our love lives, so our vision is sometimes blurred. Even the most self-aware of us have blind spots when we are in love or our relationship is troubled.

But the truth is, no matter how good the relationship, partners can benefit from new insights. And couples in troubled relationships generally need new ways to understand the source of their problems. Plus, it's just plain intriguing—and entertaining—to know more about ourselves as a lover or a spouse. For that matter, it's time well spent to get to know ourselves so that we can choose our partners more intelligently. All of us benefit by deeper information about the way we feel, think, and behave—and how we fit with other people in our lives.

The question, then, is, How do you learn about something as personal as your love life? The tests in this book are designed to give you that valuable perspective. Psychologists, sociologists, therapists, and other social scientists have spent professional lifetimes creating inventories of questions to understand every imaginable aspect of relationships.

Therapists and counselors use these tests to help them identify problem areas—and strengths—that they can highlight in their efforts to assist couples set on improving their relationships. Researchers use these tests to establish the knowledge that the social sciences have accrued regarding relationships. We have reviewed the research and clinical practice tools used to study and help relationships and have found what we consider to be the best tools for assessing relationships.

We have identified thirty-two scales, questionnaires, and inventories that you can use to evaluate your love life. The inventories we've selected can give you insight into accepting, changing, or celebrating your love life. Use them as a guide to prevent problems when things are going well, or use them when you have the sense that your relationship is unraveling.

What Will You Learn?

You'll learn about your relationship, but you'll learn about yourself, too. Each part of this book will guide you to greater insight into your unique contributions to relationships.

• Section 1: Falling in Love evaluates issues related to what kind of lover and romantic you are. Questions are raised such as: Are you comfortable with intimacy? What kind of lover are you?

• Section 2: Staying in Love and Being Close provides a relationship checkup that evaluates your overall satisfaction with your current relationship—or one you've had in the past. How satisfied are you with your relationship?

• Section 3: Key Emotional Issues focuses on respect, trust, jealousy, self-disclosure, and communication. Do you tend to save up conflict or do you solve problems as they arise? What are your relationship standards? And how do they match up with your partner's?

• Section 4: Sex with Someone You Love includes six tests about sexual knowledge, attitudes, satisfaction, communication, and affairs. Are you satisfied with the way you and your partner let each other know about your sexual desires? Are you vulnerable to an extramarital affair? Do you know the warning signs of an emotional affair?

• Section 5: Getting a Fair Deal addresses an array of fairness issues from housework, to finances, to family issues, to emotional issues. How does the household labor get divided, and how satisfied are you with it? Are you submitting to the needs of your partner—and suffering because of it?

• Section 6: Some Serious Relationship Issues raises questions about trouble spots in terms of how you relate to each other or where major problems are causing your relationship to deteriorate. Do you think you could do better than your current relationship?

These are some of the questions asked and answered by this book that are useful for individuals—as individuals— as well as for people interested in learning more about their relationships.

ABOUT THE TESTS IN THIS BOOK

We have identified state-of-the-art social-scientific tests of numerous aspects of relationships, from how you relate to others romantically to what you think your alternatives would be if your relationship ended. Not only have we spent our research careers in the study of sex and relationships; we are also steeped in the business of communicating to the public what we—and other scientists—know about sex and relationships. Therefore we have been able to identify the best available measures of your relationship and your love life. In many cases we have been able to interview the creators of these inventories about the strengths and goals of their particular measures, about the validity of the scales, and about the most useful way for individuals and couples to take these tests. Some of the tests have scoring criteria that are easy for individuals to use. Other tests, however, have scoring criteria that are particular to research rather than for use by individuals. In those cases, we used the research as a guide for how to create criteria that are meaningful to individuals and couples using these tools at home.

As you will see again and again in this book, the scoring is not about what's a good or bad relationship—that is information that no single test or set of tests in a book can give you. What the scoring provides you with are new ways to ask yourself questions about your relationship. One more thing our friends tell us about taking these tests and scoring them: A calculator will come in handy, but the calculations aren't too complex.

Sometimes people think that tests on relationships are the invention of the editors of women's (and increasingly, men's) magazines. And these magazines often do a good job of coming up with relevant questions about different aspects of their readers' love lives. However, our tests are the products of years and years of social research by the nation's top experts in couples' issues. We have striven to bring the social laboratory to your living room—or to your bedroom if you prefer.

HOW TO USE THIS BOOK

You will answer many of the tests in terms of how much or how little you feel or behave a certain way. Other tests will ask you what kind of attitudes you have toward your relationship. Several tests have open-ended response sections, so you can provide your own unique definitions of the strengths and problems in your relationship, and we have included flexible scoring schemes to fit your current situation.

Some people might want to take these tests with their partner; others might want to reflect on how they would respond, and then how their partner would respond. In still other cases, individuals may want to use these tests to understand a relationship that has ended, or to learn what their ideal relationship might look like.

Use this book as a tool to build a better relationship. It will help you imagine different ways of being in a relationship. While this book should help you recognize problems that are serious and may not change, it doesn't just focus on problems. One of the delightful things about these tests is that many identify the strengths of your relationship. Many people will learn that their positive evaluation of their relationship is right on target.

In some cases, however, these tests may lead you to consider getting additional help. Indeed, these tests should not be thought of as a substitute for getting professional help from a (qualified) psychotherapist or for taking a couples' education course. Often, therapy or counseling isn't necessary for couples. Couples can help themselves with just a bit of guidance provided by the outside points of view available in this book. Other times, couples may wish to take a couples' education course or seek individual or couples' counseling. Because you may consider this option at some point, at the end of our book you will find a list of some organizations where you can find couples' therapists or couples' education courses. This book is in no way a substitute for a professional "diagnosis" of your relationship or yourself. It is a way to gain insights into you and your partner's behavior, attitudes, and compatibility.

IT'S NOT ABOUT BEING NORMAL. NO, IT'S ABOUT MATCHING

People sometimes look to tests like these as a way of determining whether they are normal, or to find out if their relationship meets some kind of standard. In *The Love Test* you won't find that you are receiving a grade. However, you should be aware of a common theme among psychologists, sociologists, therapists, and social scientists: the theme of **matching**. Research emphasizes that what matters most for couples is that they *match* on their attitudes and styles of having a relationship. That is, if you are **both** satisfied with sexual activity once a month, your agreement on this is what matters. Yes, there are certain kinds of communication that are always destructive, and there are abuses of power in relationships that should be out-of-bounds. But when it comes to your love life, there is a wide variety of equally satisfying arrangements. There are many different ways to have a happy relationship, and many different ways to feel and experience love. Sex, too, is something that is infinitely varied. So rest assured that this book is not about one-size-fits-all, but about how well your experience and your partner's experience match up.

A final note: Some of the tests in this book are referred to by name as relating to marriage. The questionnaires, however, are used regularly for people in committed relationships who are not married. Also, some of the tests in this book include scoring that was provided by the creators of the particular tests. However, where the scoring was excessively complicated or involved creating summaries that would be useful only to researchers who are studying groups of people rather than interviewing individuals or couples, we established original guidelines to aid you in understanding your responses to the tests.

Falling in Love

What Kind of Lover Am I?

This section measures: What kind of love you are experiencing • Whether you are traditional or sex-oriented when it comes to romance • How comfortable you are with intimacy • How passionate you both are

THE LOVE ATTITUDES SCALE

This test has six sections to help you learn what your style of loving is. Answer how strongly you agree with each statement as it relates to your current relationship (with a lover, significant other, or spouse). If you aren't in a relationship right now, think of your ideal relationship and your beliefs about relationships in general. To complete the test, indicate the extent to which you agree with each item using the scale below:

5	4	3	2	1
strongly agree	agree	neutral	disagree	strongly disagree

After you take the test you will learn what your love style is. The subscores you will have when you're done represent different styles of loving: Eros, Ludus, Storge, Pragma, Mania, and Agape. These categories—and these Greek words for love—will be explained when you're done.

PART 1: LOVE STATEMENTS

How much do you agree?

1. My partner and I were attracted to each other immediately when we first met. _____

2. My partner and I have the right physical "chemistry" between us. _____

3. Our lovemaking is very intense and satisfying. _____

4. I feel that my partner and I were meant for each other. _____

5. My partner and I became physically or emotionally involved rather quickly. _____

6. My partner and I really understand each other. _____

7. My partner fits my ideal standards of physical beauty/handsomeness. _____

Eros Subscore _____

8. I try to keep my partner a little uncertain about my commitment to him/her. _____

9. I believe that what my partner doesn't know about me won't hurt him/her. _____

10. I have sometimes had to keep two of my partners from finding out about each other. _____

11. I can get over love affairs pretty easily and quickly. _____

12. My partner would get upset if s/he knew of some of the things I've done with other people. _____

13. When my partner gets too dependent on me, I want to back off a little. _____

14. I enjoy playing the "game of love" with a number of different partners. _____

Ludus Subscore _____

15. It is hard to say exactly where the friendship ends and love begins. _____

16. I cannot love unless I've first had caring for a while. _____

17. I still have good friendships with almost everyone with whom I have ever been involved in a love relationship. _____

18. The best kind of love grows out of a long friendship. _____

19. It is hard to say exactly when my partner and I fell in love. _____

20. Love is really a deep friendship, not a mysterious, mystical emotion. _____

21. My most satisfying love relationships have developed from good relationships. _____

Storge Subscore _____

PART 2: LOVE BEHAVIORS

**How
much
do you
agree?**

22. I consider what a person is going to become
in life before I commit myself to him/her.   _____

23. I try to plan my life carefully before
choosing a partner.   _____

24. It is best to love someone with a similar
background.   _____

25. A main consideration in choosing a partner
is how s/he reflects on my family.   _____

26. An important factor in choosing a partner is
whether or not s/he will be a good parent.   _____

27. One consideration in choosing a partner is
how s/he will reflect on my career.   _____

28. Before getting very involved with anyone,
I try to figure out how compatible his/her
hereditary background is with mine in case
we ever have children.   _____

Pragma Subscore   _____

29. When things aren't right with my partner
and me, my stomach gets upset.   _____

30. When my love affairs break up, I get so
depressed that I have even thought of suicide.   _____

31. Sometimes I get so excited about being in
love that I can't sleep.   _____

32. When my partner doesn't pay attention to me, I feel sick all over. _____

33. When I am in love, I have trouble concentrating on anything else. _____

34. I cannot relax if I suspect that my partner is with someone else. _____

35. If my partner ignores me for a while, I sometimes do stupid things to get his/her attention back. _____

Mania Subscore _____

36. I try to use my own strength to help my partner through difficult times. _____

37. I would rather suffer myself than let my partner suffer. _____

38. I cannot be happy unless I place my partner's happiness before my own. _____

39. I am usually willing to sacrifice my own wishes to let my partner achieve his/hers. _____

40. Whatever I own is my partner's to use as s/he chooses. _____

41. When my partner gets angry with me, I still love him/her fully and unconditionally. _____

42. I would endure all things for the sake of my partner. _____

Agape Subscore _____

Scoring and Evaluation

For each of the subsections, add up the total and enter it below. These subsection scores are associated with three main love styles that are related to how you *feel*:

1. **Eros (passionate) score:**   _____
2. **Ludus (playful) score:**   _____
3. **Storge (friendship) score:**   _____

and three secondary styles that are related to how you *act*:

4. **Pragma (practical) score:**   _____
5. **Mania (intense) score:**   _____
6. **Agape (selfless) score:**   _____

The range for each subscore is from 7 through 35.

Identify your love style by finding the highest score in the first set of love styles and the highest score in the second set of love styles.

What do your love style scores mean? These love styles may change over a lifetime, but not always. These categories give you a sense of the kind of lover you tend to be—even if you aren't in a relationship right now. If you are in a relationship, they also help describe what you are like and how you behave in that relationship. Consider asking your partner to take this test, too, and then see how well you match.

What do these categories mean? The terms are derived from six Greek words for different kinds of love:

• *Eros* stands for passionate love. In researching this test, the authors found that people who reported that they are currently in love were particularly likely to be identified with Eros. Eros involves strong physical preferences and responses to a lover, and a lot of commitment is involved. Eros was the most common feeling among respondents in recent research on Love Attitudes.

• *Ludus* stands for game-playing love. People who score high in this category approach love as an interactional game—even if it sometimes involves deception. Ludus types may even be wary of closeness. Men were more likely to approach love as a game, although men and women were pretty similar in this regard. People who have never been in love and those who have been in love again, and again, and again tended to fit well into this category, while people who have been in love only once or twice were not as likely to belong in this category. Ludus was the least common feeling among respondents in recent research.

• If you scored high on *Storge*, you have an inclination to link love and friendship. It is an enduring kind of love, but it is not a particularly passionate kind of love. Storge was less common than Eros, but much more common than Ludus in recent research.

The next three types are subtypes that reflect how you behave regarding your feelings.

• If you scored high on *Pragma*, you are a rational thinker. You focus on finding a lover who has the kind of qualities that you prefer; you may even have a plan about the ideal relationship before you find the lover of your dreams. Among the second set of love attitudes, Pragma was the least common.

• *Mania* may be what sometimes is called puppy love—

since it is particularly common among adolescents (although plenty of older lovers can be Manic). There is a high degree of uncertainty about the lover and a lot of activity around seeking to fix that uncertainty.

• *Agape* is rare in its purest form, although it received the highest score among the second three Love Attitudes. Agape is selfless love, the kind that involves giving without taking, and may only appear in its true form in parents of small children—and then perhaps only on occasion.

If you take this test with your partner, matching is ideal. If your scores for each "love type" are less than 12 points apart, you should consider that matching.

From Clyde Hendrick and Susan Hendrick, "A Theory and Method of Love" (Department of Psychology, Texas Tech University), *Journal of Personality and Social Psychology* 50 (1986): 392–402. Copyright ©1986 American Psychological Associaton. Reprinted with permission of the authors and APA. The authors also have a revised, relationship-specific version.

TRADITIONAL OR SEXUAL? THE ROMANTIC TOP TWENTY QUIZ

Directions: Review the list of twenty top romantic activities below and indicate, using the scale of one to five, how important each activity is in your ideal romantic relationship.

1	2	3	4	5
not at all important	unimportant	neither unimportant or important	important	extremely important

ROMANTIC ACTIVITY

How impor-
tant is
this to
you?

1. Saying I love you* _____
2. Having sex♠ _____
3. Undressing each other♠ _____
4. Engaging in sexual foreplay♠ _____
5. Lying about in front of a fire* _____
6. Cuddling* _____
7. Climaxing at the same time♠ _____
8. Having spontaneous sex♠ _____
9. Walking on the beach* _____
10. Taking a shower together♠ _____
11. Walking in the moonlight* _____
12. Hearing "I love you"* _____
13. Receiving a special card* _____
14. Being undressed by the other♠ _____
15. Sharing hopes and dreams* _____
16. Touching each other* _____
17. Finding love notes from each other* _____
18. Being together out in nature* _____
19. French kissing♠ _____
20. Sharing a Jacuzzi or hot tub♠ _____

Scoring and Evaluation
Once you have answered all of the questions, create two
sums.

1. For *Traditional Romantic Sum*, add together responses followed by *:_____.
   The range of possible scores (if you answered everything) is 11 to 55.

In the research on the "Romantic Top Twenty," about two-thirds of respondents scored between 41 and 53 on the traditional items. If your traditional-romantic score was below 30 then you are not particularly interested in traditional romance.

2. For *Sexual Romantic Sum*, add together responses followed by ♠:_____.
   The range of possible scores (if you answered everything) is 9 to 45.

In the research on the "Romantic Top Twenty," about two-thirds of respondents scored between 29 and 40 on the sexual items. If your sexual romantic score was below 24 then romance isn't sexualized for you.

This information can also help you determine how romantic you are, overall. You can obtain your total romantic score by adding together the two sums; the range is between 20 and 100. Between 70 and 93 is similar to what most people score, and that is pretty romantic. A score above 93 is very romantic, indeed. A score below 70, however, does not necessarily mean that you are *unromantic*. It may mean that there are other things that you feel are romantic. The researchers who determined the "Top Twenty" also looked at other items related to marriage and family, religion, and stability.

Based on research reported in Daniel Prentice, Nancy Briggs, and David Bradley, "Romantic Attitudes of American University Students," *Psychological Reports* 53 (1983): 815–22. Reprinted by permission of the authors.

RISK IN INTIMACY INVENTORY

irections: Answer the following 10 questions by filling in the answer most consistent with your point of view:

6 strongly agree   3 mildly disagree
5 agree   2 disagree
4 mildly agree   1 strongly disagree

Statement   **Strength**

1. It is dangerous to get really close to people. _____
2. I prefer that people keep their distance from me. _____
3. I'm afraid to get really close to someone because I might get hurt. _____

4. At best, I can handle only one or two close
   friendships at a time.   _____

5. I find it difficult to trust other people.   _____

6. I avoid intimacy.   _____

7. Being close to other people makes me feel
   afraid.   _____

8. I'm hesitant to share personal information
   about myself.   _____

9. Being close to people is a risky business.   _____

10. The most important thing to consider in a
    relationship is whether I might get hurt.   _____

Risk in Intimacy Score [range: 10–60]:   _____

Scoring and Evaluation

Simply add up the values of your responses to obtain your
Risk in Intimacy score. The higher your score, the more
uncomfortable you are with intimacy. Based on our
evaluation of the research, if you have a score below 20,
then intimacy isn't a barrier to getting involved for you.
But if you have a score above 36, this is a trouble spot
for you.

People who score high on this tend to view intimacy (or
getting close to another person) as risky to themselves.
High scorers are more likely to distance themselves from
others and have few friends. They are cautious about getting involved and take things slowly when they do get
involved in an intimate relationship. In other words, close
relationships aren't impossible for people who are high on
"Risk in Intimacy"; but they may take more time to get
really close to their significant other.

PASSIONATE LOVE SCALE

Directions: Think of the person you love most passionately right now: your significant other. (If you are not in love, think of the most recent person you have been in love with.) Using the scale indicated below, identify the number that most closely represents the way you felt when your feelings were most intense about this person.

9	8	7	6	5	4	3	2	1
definitely true			**moderately true**			**not at all true**		

1. I would feel deep despair if _____ left me. _____
2. Sometimes I feel I can't control my thoughts. They are obsessively on _____ . _____

3. I feel happy when I am doing something to make _____ happy.   _____

4. I would rather be with _____ than anyone else.   _____

5. I'd get jealous if I thought _____ were falling in love with someone else.   _____

6. I yearn to know all about _____.   _____

7. I want _____ : physically, emotionally, and mentally.   _____

8. I have an endless appetite for affection from _____.   _____

9. For me, _____ is the perfect romantic partner.   _____

10. I sense my body responding when _____ touches me.   _____

11. _____ always seems to be on my mind.   _____

12. I want _____ to know me—my thoughts, my fears, my hopes.   _____

13. I eagerly look for signs indicating _____'s desire for me.   _____

14. I possess a powerful attraction for _____ .   _____

Score [range: 14–126]:   _____

Scoring and Evaluation

The higher your score, the more passionate a lover you are. Although passionate love tends to be associated with youth and adolescence (that delicious puppy love!), people of all ages can be passionate lovers. Although passion may decline over the length of a relationship, it does not disappear.

What's the difference between passionate love and the infatuation we call "puppy love"? According to a number of researchers, based on work conducted over the past thirty years, you cannot tell the difference. Only time will distinguish the two. By examining how well your love measures up under other love tests, however, you may be able to learn more about the features of your love life besides the passion you experience for your beloved.

Originally presented by the creators, sociologists Elaine Hatfield, Ph.D. (University of Hawaii), and Susan Sprecher, Ph.D.(Illinois State University), in *Journal of Adolescence* (1986); as reported in Hatfield and Richard Rapson, *Love, Sex, and Intimacy: Their Psychology, Biology, and History* (HarperCollins, 1993). Reprinted by permission of the authors.

Staying in Love and Being Close

A Relationship Checkup

This section measures: How close the two of you are • How well you feel your relationship is going • How well you know each other • How satisfied you are and how well your marriage meets your goals • How much love and respect you and your partner feel

RELATIONSHIP
CLOSENESS
INVENTORY

This inventory includes four parts that evaluate three aspects of your time spent with a significant other: Frequency, Diversity, and Strength. They can be evaluated to learn more about how close you and your partner are.

Directions: This test evaluates your closest, most intimate relationship: your lover, your spouse, your partner in life. We refer to this person as your *significant other* (s.o.). The questions are in reference to that relationship.

Part I. This section is about how much time you spend with your *significant other* and what kinds of things you do together. Think back over the past week and write in the average amount of time per day that you spent alone with

your s.o., when no one else was around. If you spent no time
with your s.o. in some of the time periods, fill in zeroes.

1. During the past week, what is the average
   amount of time, per day, that you spent alone
   with your *s.o.* in the morning, between
   waking and noon?
   _____ hours _____ minutes   minutes: _____

2. During the past week, what is the average
   amount of time, per day, that you spent alone
   with your *s.o.* in the afternoon, between noon
   and 6 P.M.?
   _____ hours _____ minutes   minutes: _____

3. During the past week, what is the average
   amount of time per day that you spent alone
   with your *s.o.* in the evening, between around
   6 .P.M. and bedtime?
   _____ hours _____ minutes   minutes: _____

Subscore 1 (total minutes):   _____

Part II. In the past week, which of the following activities
did you do alone with your *s.o.* (check all that apply):

____ did laundry   ____ went to a movie

____ prepared a meal   ____ ate a meal

____ watched TV   ____ participated in a

____ went to an auction/   sporting activity

     antique show   ____ outdoor recre-

____ attended a lecture   ation (such as sail-

     (not school-related)   ing, biking)

____ went to a restaurant

____ went to a grocery store

____ went for a walk/drive

____ discussed things of
a personal nature

____ went to a museum
or art show

____ planned a party or
social event

____ attended a class

____ went on a trip
(vacation or a week-
end away)

____ cleaned house or
apartment

____ went to church or a
religious function

____ worked on homework

____ engaged in sexual
relations

____ discussed things
of a nonpersonal
nature

____ went to a clothing
store

____ talked on the phone

____ went to a play

____ went to a bar

____ visited family

____ visited friends

____ went to a
department, book,
hardware store (or
something similar)

____ played cards or
a board game

____ attending a sport-
ing event

____ exercised (jog-
ging, aerobics, et
cetera)

____ went on an out-
ing (a picnic,
beach, zoo, winter
carnival, et cetera)

____ wilderness
activity (hunting,
hiking, fishing)

____ went to a concert

____ went dancing

____ went to a party

____ played music/sang

Subscore 2 (total activities):   _____

Part III. The questions in this section pertain to the amount of influence your significant other has over your thoughts, feelings, and behavior. For each of the following statements, circle the number in the column that fits your response.

	Strongly Agree	Agree	Slightly Agree	Neutral	Slightly Disagree	Disagree	Strongly Disagree
[My s.o.] will influence my future financial security.	1	2	3	4	5	6	7
[My s.o.] does not influence everyday things in my life.	7	6	5	4	3	2	1
[My s.o.] influences important things in my life.	1	2	3	4	5	6	7
[My s.o.] influences which parties and other social events I attend.	1	2	3	4	5	6	7

	Strongly Agree	Agree	Slightly Agree	Neutral	Slightly Disagree	Disagree	Strongly Disagree
[My s.o.] influences the extent to which I accept responsibilities in our relationship.	1	2	3	4	5	6	7
[My s.o.] does not influence how much time I spend doing household work.	7	6	5	4	3	2	1
[My s.o.] does not influence how I choose to spend my money.	7	6	5	4	3	2	1
[My s.o.] so influences the way I feel about myself.	1	2	3	4	5	6	7

	Strongly Agree	Agree	Slightly Agree	Neutral	Slightly Disagree	Disagree	Strongly Disagree
[My s.o.] does not influence my moods.	7	6	5	4	3	2	1
[My s.o.] influences the basic values that I hold.	1	2	3	4	5	6	7
[My s.o.] does not influence the opinions that I have of other important people in my life.	7	6	5	4	3	2	1
[My s.o.] does not influence when I see and the amount of time I spend with my family.	7	6	5	4	3	2	1
[My s.o.] influences when I see and the amount of time I spend with my friends.	1	2	3	4	5	6	7

	Strongly Agree	Agree	Slightly Agree	Neutral	Slightly Disagree	Disagree	Strongly Disagree
[My s.o.] does not influence which of my friends I see.	7	6	5	4	3	2	1
[My s.o.] does not influence the type of career I have.	7	6	5	4	3	2	1
[My s.o.] influences or will influence how much time I devote to my career.	1	2	3	4	5	6	7
[My s.o.] does not influence my chances of getting a good job in the future.	7	6	5	4	3	2	1
[My s.o.] influences the way I feel about the future.	1	2	3	4	5	6	7

	Strongly Agree	Agree	Slightly Agree	Neutral	Slightly Disagree	Disagree	Strongly Disagree
[My s.o.] does not have the capacity to influence how I act in various situations.	7	6	5	4	3	2	1
[My s.o.] influences and contributes to my overall happiness.	1	2	3	4	5	6	7
[My s.o.] does not influence my present financial security.	7	6	5	4	3	2	1
[My s.o.] influences how I spend my free time.	1	2	3	4	5	6	7
[My s.o.] influences when I see him/her and the amount of time we spend together.	1	2	3	4	5	6	7

	Strongly Agree	Agree	Slightly Agree	Neutral	Slightly Disagree	Disagree	Strongly Disagree
[My s.o.] does not influence how I dress.	7	6	5	4	3	2	1
[My s.o.] influences how I decorate my home.	1	2	3	4	5	6	7
[My s.o.] does not influence where I live.	7	6	5	4	3	2	1
[My s.o.] influences what I watch on TV.	1	2	3	4	5	6	7
Subscore 3 (sum of responses): _____							

Part IV. Finally, indicate how much your significant other affects your future plans and goals. Using the seven point scale below, indicate the answers that are consistent with your response.

1   **2**   **3**   **4**   **5**   **6**   **7**
not at all   **neutral**   **a great extent**

1. My vacation plans: _____

2. My marriage plans*: _____

3. My plans to have children: _____

4. My plans to make major investments: _____

5. My plans to join a club, social organization,
   church, et cetera: _____

6. My school- or job-related plans: _____

7. My plans for achieving a particular standard
   of living: _____

   *(If you are already married, indicate 7)

Subscore 4 (sum of responses):   _____

Scoring and Evaluation

• Calculate your Subscore 1 by adding together the amount of time you spend alone with your significant other in minutes. (If you spend one hour and thirty minutes together then you would indicate 90 minutes, for example.) This is your *Frequency Score*. In other words, this is a measure of how much alone-time you have with your significant other during the week. Alone-time is an important feature of intimate relationships, but it does not stand alone without diversity and strength.

• Calculate your Subscore 2 by counting the number of different activities you do with your significant other. This score is your *Diversity Score*. This score summarizes how many different things you and your significant other do together. Common interests and shared activity are an important aspect of enduring, close relationships.

• Calculate Subscores 3 and 4 by adding up the value for each question. Once you have calculated these subscores, you may add them together to obtain your *Strength Score*. This score measures the amount of influence your significant other has on your life plans, the things you do, and the expectations you have of the future. Some research shows that this score has the strongest association with love of the three scores available.

The creators of the Relationship Closeness Inventory, Professor Ellen Berscheid (University of Minnesota) and her colleagues, established a ten-point scale for each of the three categories in the test. The higher your ten-point score, the closer you and your significant other are with respect to frequency, diversity, or strength. For each sub-score, find where you fit in best in the following column of scores. Then identify your scale score by looking across the row to the right-hand column. For example, if your diversity score is 7 to 9, then your scale score is a 5.

Frequency Score (in Minutes)	Diversity Score	Strength Score	Scale Score
0–12	0	34–53	1
13–48	1	54–73	2
49–108	2–3	74–93	3
109–192	4–6	94–113	4
193–300	7–9	114–133	5
301–432	10–13	134–153	6
433–588	14–18	154–173	7
589–768	19–24	174–193	8
769–972	25–30	194–213	9
973–1200	31–38	214–238	10

Frequency Score:	_____	**Scale Score:**	_____
Diversity Score:	_____	**Scale Score:**	_____
Strength Score:	_____	**Scale Score:**	_____
Scale Sum:			_____

Finally, Berscheid and colleagues created a sum of the three scale scores and found that they were associated with different lengths of romantic relationships. (They also examined non-romantic relationships; but these tend to dissolve more slowly even if they are not particularly good. While friends can drift apart, lovers typically experience a more timely breakup.) To see how you fit into their observations, add together your scale score for each column.

How does your scale score compare with what the researchers found? If your combined score is 11 or lower, you are similar to those people who had an early breakup (within three months). If your combined score is between 11 and 13, you are similar to those people who broke up in 3 to 6 months. People with scores around 15 or higher were people whose relationships lasted through the study and beyond.

What is particularly useful about this scale is that it emphasizes both what you do and how you experience influence from your partner. In related research, social scientists have observed that doing things together and being closely involved in each other's lives is closely related to satisfaction and a lower likelihood that you'll break up.

RELATIONSHIP ASSESSMENT SCALE

This brief quiz provides you with a subjective evaluation of the quality of your love relationship—from your own point of view.

Directions: Using the scale below, please indicate which number best answers each question.

5	4	3	2	1
extremely well		average		poorly

1. How well does your partner meet your needs? _____
2. In general, how satisfied are you with your relationship? _____

3. How good is your relationship compared to most? _____

4. How often do you wish you hadn't gotten into this relationship?* _____

5. To what extent has your relationship met your original expectations? _____

6. How much do you love your partner? _____

7. How many problems are there in your relationship?* _____

Reverse score

Scoring

To find where you fit on the Relationship Assessment Scale, *first* reverse score questions 4 and 7. To "reverse score," subtract your response from 6. (If you responded 2, for example, then your answer is 6 minus 2, or 4.) This means 1 becomes 5; 2 becomes 4; 3 remains the same; 4 becomes 2; and 5 becomes 1. Then add together all seven responses and divide by seven. Your score should be between 1 and 5. As you can see, the higher your score, the more positively you see your relationship. Sum:_____÷7=_____score

The researchers who developed this scale have found that dating couples score a little bit higher on average than couples who are in long-term, committed relationships and marriage. Part of this may be because when couples have children, their score on this test will, on average, be a little bit lower than when they do not have children. The presence of children is more complicated, though, because not only do a significant percentage of couples with children score lower than average on this test, but some couples with children will score exceptionally high. Below are percentiles based on reviewing five studies that used this quiz.

3.2 . . . . . 10th percentile
3.3 . . . . . 20th percentile
4.1 . . . . . 40th percentile
4.8 . . . . . 80th percentile
4.9 . . . . . 90th percentile

If you and your partner are in the 40th percentile or higher, your relationship is, overall, satisfactory to you. If you or your partner is in the 20th percentile or lower, you may want to think about which parts of the relationship you'd like to see improved.

It is interesting to note that from the research that used this scale it was determined that there are no gender differences in terms of relationship happiness, according to this test. That is, men and women tend to report similar levels of relationship satisfaction—whether they are dating, married, or married with children. The only category where there is a small gender difference is among couples in therapy. For couples who are seeking therapy, the women are less satisfied with the relationship than the men are.

Reprinted by permission of Clyde Hendrick and Susan S. Hendrick. Drs. Hendrick are in the Psychology Department at Texas Tech University and the authors of *Romantic Love* (Thousand Oaks, Calif.: Sage Books, 1992).

ABBREVIATED
RELATIONSHIP
INVENTORY

The following test was derived from an earlier, longer relationship inventory. It is unique because it evaluates *how well you feel your partner knows you and understands you*. The feeling of "being known" to a lover—as well as the feeling of really "knowing" your lover—are key components of a strong love relationship. This is a wonderful test to ask your partner to take so that you can learn how well s/he feels that you know him/her, too. If your scores are not as high as you would like, the test may give you ideas on ways you might be able to create more closeness with your partner.

Directions: For each of the following statements, circle the number in the column that fits your response to each one.

Intimacy Statements	agree strongly	agree moderately	neutral	disagree moderately	disagree strongly
1. My partner nearly always knows exactly what I mean.	5	4	3	2	1
2. My partner usually senses or realizes what I am feeling.	5	4	3	2	1
3. My partner realizes what I mean even when I have difficulty saying it.	5	4	3	2	1
4. My partner usually understands the whole meaning of what I say to him/her.	5	4	3	2	1
5. My partner appreciates exactly how the things I experience feel to me.	5	4	3	2	1

Subscore 1 (sum of responses) [range: 5–25]: _____

Intimacy Statements	agree strongly	agree moderately	neutral	disagree moderately	disagree strongly
6. My partner respects me as a person.	5	4	3	2	1
7. My partner feels a true liking for me.	5	4	3	2	1
8. My partner finds me rather dull and uninteresting.	1	2	3	4	5
9. My partner cares for me.	5	4	3	2	1
10. My partner is friendly and warm with me.	5	4	3	2	1
11. My partner feels a deep affection for me.	5	4	3	2	1

Subscore 2 (sum of responses) [range: 6–30]: ____

12. My partner expresses his/her true impressions and feelings with me.	5	4	3	2	1

Intimacy Statements	agree strongly	agree moderately	neutral	disagree moderately	disagree strongly
13. My partner is usually willing to express whatever is actually on his/her mind with me, particularly feelings about our relationship.	5	4	3	2	1
14. My partner is openly him/herself in our relationship.	5	4	3	2	1
15. There are times when I feel that my partner's outward response to me is quite different from the way s/he feels underneath.	1	2	3	4	5

Subscore 3 (sum of responses) [range: 4–20]:___

Total Score (sum of subscores) [range:15–75]:____

Scoring and Evaluation

Based on our review of the research, the following guidelines will help you assess your total score:

- 55+: you are doing very well.
- 40–54: you are doing all right, no major problems.
- 30–39: you may want to seek strategies to feel closer to each other.
- 29 or below: it is a good idea to find some ways to feel closer.

The Subscores tell you about three main areas of closeness and intimacy.

Subscore 1 evaluates *understanding and empathy*. The higher the score, the more you experience your partner's empathy for you.

Subscore 2 evaluates *regard or esteem*. The higher the score, the more highly you feel your partner respects you.

Subscore 3 evaluates *congruence*, or the extent to which you and your partner are "on the same page" about emotional issues and the extent to which you are open to each other. Again, the higher this score, the more congruent or connected you and your partner are.

Based on a questionnaire developed by Professors Walter Schumm, Stephan Bollman, and Tony Jurich, Department of Human Ecology, Kansas State University. Reprinted by permission of the authors.

Aspects of Marital Satisfaction Questionnaire

Directions: For each of the 16 aspects of marriage listed below, select the rating from the scales provided that answers the questions "How satisfied are you with each of these aspects of your marriage?" and "How important to your marriage is each of these aspects?

Satisfaction Scale (How *satisfied* are you with each of these aspects of your marriage?)

5: Enthusiastic—it could not be any
   better   _____
4: Quite satisfied   _____
3: It's all right, I guess—I can't
   complain   _____

2: A little disappointed—it could be
   better   _____
1: Really disappointed—not what I
   expected   _____

Importance Scale (How *important* to your marriage is
each of these aspects?)

6: Absolutely essential   3: Moderately important
5: Extremely important   2: Slightly important
4: Very important   1: Not at all important

Aspect of Marriage	Satisfaction	Importance
1. Opportunity to raise children		
2. Enjoying sexual relations with spouse		
3. Understanding by spouse of your problems and feelings		
4. Standard of living—kind of house, car, et cetera		
5. Finding sex with your spouse to be exciting		
6. Expressions of love and affection by spouse		
7. Household tasks which are done by spouse		

Aspect of Marriage	Satisfaction	Importance
8. Having sexual relations as often as desired		
9. Companionship in doing things with spouse		
10. Having sexual relations bound up with love and affection		
11. Having fun with spouse		
12. Romantic experiences with spouse		
13. Being respected by spouse		
14. Having similar intellectual interests with spouse		
15. Being in love with spouse		
16. Self-confidence or self-esteem enhanced by spouse		
Total (sum of responses):		
Range	16–80	16–96

Scoring and Evaluation

To evaluate your relationship *Satisfaction*, add together your responses in the left-hand column. The higher your score, the more satisfied you are in your relationship. A score of 32 or lower may be a sign that you want to find ways to improve your relationship. The satisfaction questions on this test focus on some of the most central goals people have in their committed relationships. Instead of tapping your feelings—which are important too—this questionnaire is a measure of how well your relationship measures up to your aspirations in marriage.

To discover more about how your marriage measures up to your aspirations, you can use the *Importance* score. The *Importance* score will spotlight your satisfaction with your most valued aspects of marriage. To determine your level of satisfaction with the things that matter most to you, find the questions for which your individual *Importance* score was 4, 5, or 6, and add together the *Satisfaction* scores for those same items. Enter this number below:

(A) Total Satisfaction score for high-importance responses:

_____

Now count up how many of your Importance scores were a 4 or higher.

(B) Total number of Importance responses of 4, 5, or 6:   _____

Now divide the number in (A) by the number in (B). The answer should be between 1 and 5. You can use the satisfaction scale above to see how satisfied you are with the areas of your marriage that are *most important* to you. If this score is above 3, then your satisfaction with the things that matter most to you is high or very high.

The other value of the Importance score is to compare the most important items to your partner's. Feeling satisfied with higher importance items is what's really important for sustaining a happy and satisfying relationship. Identifying the items of greatest importance to you or to your partner can guide you both to those aspects of your relationship that need attention—to change or to learn to accept—in order to improve your satisfaction.

LOVE AND RESPECT
QUESTIONNAIRE

This is a very good test to ask your partner to take as well. You can learn whether or not you are successful at making your partner feel loved and respected; and s/he can learn whether you feel loved and respected.

Directions: Answer true or false to each of the following statements, depending on whether it is true or mostly true, or false or mostly false. If you'd like, ask your partner to take it too.

Statement about the Love and Respect in My Relationship	My Response	Partner's Response
1. My partner seeks out my opinions.	T or F	T or F
2. My partner cares about my feelings.	T or F	T or F
3. I don't feel ignored very often.	T or F	T or F
4. We touch each other a lot.	T or F	T or F
5. We listen to each other.	T or F	T or F
6. We respect each other's ideas.	T or F	T or F
7. We are affectionate toward each other.	T or F	T or F
8. I feel that my partner takes good care of me.	T or F	T or F
9. What I say counts.	T or F	T or F
10. I am important in our decisions.	T or F	T or F
11. There's lots of love in our relationship.	T or F	T or F
12. We are genuinely interested in one another.	T or F	T or F
13. I just love spending time with my partner.	T or F	T or F

Statement about the Love and Respect in My Relationship	My Response	Partner's Response
14. We are very good friends.	T or F	T or F
15. Even during rough times, we can be empathetic.	T or F	T or F
16. My partner is considerate of my viewpoint.	T or F	T or F
17. My partner finds me physically attractive.	T or F	T or F
18. My partner expresses warmth towards me.	T or F	T or F
19. I feel included in my partner's life.	T or F	T or F
20. My partner admires me.	T or F	T or F
Total Number of True Answers	Me:	Partner:

Scoring and Evaluation

Count up the number of true answers. If your score is below 7, then you probably are not feeling enough love and respect in your relationship. (If your partner's score is below 7, the same may be true for him/her.) If you have a score above 14, you seem to share love and respect with your partner. Keep it up, and remember that respect is a crucial component in good relationships, and it helps to sustain the bond through bad times and good.

KEY EMOTIONAL ISSUES

THIS SECTION ADDRESSES KEY EMOTIONAL ISSUES FOR COUPLES, INCLUDING: HOW MUCH TRUST YOU FEEL • WHAT KINDS OF JEALOUSY, IF ANY, YOU AND YOUR PARTNER EXPERIENCE • HOW COMFORTABLE YOU ARE WITH SELF-DISCLOSURE • HOW WILLING YOU ARE TO SHARE DARK SECRETS ABOUT YOURSELF • WHAT STANDARDS ARE MOST IMPORTANT TO YOU AND YOUR PARTNER, AND HOW WELL YOU MATCH • HOW YOU RESPOND TO EACH OTHER WHEN YOU DISAGREE

DYADIC TRUST SCALE

"**D**yadic trust" means the trust you and your partner feel in your relationship. Higher levels of trust are associated with love, self-disclosure (which will be discussed later in this section), and the security of the relationship. Trust is an important component of intimacy, especially beyond the "honeymoon" stage of romance. And it tends to be high when commitment is high.

Directions: Circle the number in the column that fits your response to each statement below. If you feel comfortable, ask your partner to do the same. If not, you may want to think about how your partner would respond to these questions.

Trust Statements	strongly agree	agree	mildly agree	neutral	mildly disagree	disagree	strongly disagree
My partner is primarily interested in his (her) own welfare.	1	2	3	4	5	6	7
There are times when my partner cannot be trusted.	1	2	3	4	5	6	7
My partner is perfectly honest and truthful with me.	7	6	5	4	3	2	1
I feel that I can trust my partner completely.	7	6	5	4	3	2	1
My partner is truly sincere in his/her promises.	7	6	5	4	3	2	1
I feel my partner does not show me enough consideration.	1	2	3	4	5	6	7

Trust Statements	strongly agree	agree	mildly agree	neutral	mildly disagree	disagree	strongly disagree
My partner treats me fairly and justly.	7	6	5	4	3	2	1
I feel that my partner can be counted on to help me.	7	6	5	4	3	2	1

Sum of Scores: _____

Scoring and Evaluation

Add together your response for each of the 8 questions. Your score should be between 8 and 56. The higher your score, the higher level of trust you experience in your relationship.

How do you compare to others in your situation? Based on research that established that the questions on this test really do measure trust, researchers found the following averages:

Relationship Type	Average Trust Score	Range*
Separated/Divorced	27	20–34
Ex-Dating Partner	41	34–48
Casual Dating	44	37–51
Exclusively Dating	47	40 +

Relationship Type	Average Trust Score	Range*
Engaged or Cohabiting	48	41+
Longer Married	49	42+
Newlyweds	49.5	42.5+

*Range determined by authors, based on our review of research.

Robert Larzelere and Ted Huston, "The Dyadic Trust Scale: Toward Understanding Interpersonal Trust in Close Relationships," *Journal of Marriage and the Family* (August): 595–604. Copyright © 1980 by the National Council on Family Relations, 3989 Central Ave., NE, #550, Minneapolis, MN 55421. Reprinted by permission of NCFR.

MULTIDIMENSIONAL
JEALOUSY SCALE

What is romantic jealousy? Some researchers think it is an emotional reaction; others think that it is not a single emotion but a combination of negative emotions. In jealousy-provoking situations some people might express anger, while others may experience hurt feelings.

What constitutes a jealousy-provoking situation? Typically it is something that threatens your relationship—or makes you *feel* threatened. As you will see, this test looks at three different parts of jealousy that researchers define as thoughts, feelings, and behaviors. While jealous feelings may be a healthy part of a loving relationship, jealous thoughts and behaviors can indicate a problem.

Directions: This test gives you an idea of the kinds of jealousy you might experience as well as how strong that jealousy is. Think about the person you are married to or romantically involved with (your "significant other"); if you aren't involved right now, think about your most recent relationship. Respond to questions 1–16 using the scale provided below, and record your responses in the boxes after each statement.

1	2	3	4	5	6	7
never			sometimes			all the time

How often do you have the following thoughts about your "significant other"?

1. I suspect that [my s.o.] is secretly seeing someone else. _____

2. I am worried that someone may be chasing after [my s.o.]. _____

3. I suspect that [my s.o.] may be attracted to someone else. _____

4. I suspect that [my s.o.] may be physically intimate with another person behind my back. _____

5. I think that some people may be romantically interested in [my s.o.]. _____

6. I am worried that someone is trying to seduce [my s.o.]. _____

7. I think that [my s.o.] is secretly developing an intimate relationship with someone else. _____

8. I suspect that [my s.o.] is crazy about men/women. _____

Subscore 1 (sum of responses): _____

How often do you engage in the following behaviors?

9. I look through [my s.o.]'s drawers, handbag, or pockets.   _____

10. I call [my s.o.] unexpectedly just to see if s/he is there.   _____

11. I question [my s.o.] about previous or present romantic relationships.   _____

12. I say something nasty about another person if [my s.o.] shows an interest in that person.   _____

13. I question [my s.o.] about his/her telephone calls.   _____

14. I question [my s.o.] about his or her where-abouts.   _____

15. I join in whenever I see [my s.o.] talking to someone who could be considered a roman-tic option.   _____

16. I pay [my s.o.] a surprise visit just to see who is with him/her.   _____

Subscore 2 (sum of responses):   _____

Respond to questions 17–24 using the following 1-7 scale provided below.

1	2	3	4	5	6	7
very pleased		neither pleased nor displeased				very upset

How would you emotionally react to the following situations?

17. [My s.o.] comments to me on how great looking a particular person is. _____

18 [My s.o.] shows a great deal of interest or excitement in talking to someone new. _____

19 [My s.o.] smiles in a very friendly manner at someone else. _____

20. Someone else is trying to get close to [my s.o.] all the time. _____

21. [My s.o.] is flirting with someone else. _____

22. Someone is dating [my s.o.]. _____

23. [My s.o.] hugs and kisses someone else. _____

24. [My s.o.] works very closely with someone else who could be a romantic candidate (in school or at work). _____

Subscore 3 (sum of responses): _____

Scoring and Evaluation

Evaluate each subscale by adding together the responses to 1–8 for Subscore 1; 9–16 for Subscore 2; and 17–24 for Subscore 3.

Subscore 1 [jealous thoughts]: _____ (range: 8–56)
Subscore 2 [jealous behaviors]: _____ (range: 8–56)
Subscore 3 [jealous feelings]: _____ (range: 8–56)
Total Jealousy: _____ (range: 24–168)

Overall, the higher your score, the more jealous you tend to be. Our review of the research helped us to create the following scoring guidelines:

• 89 or lower: you feel secure and trusting in your relationship.

• 90–109: you feel fairly secure and trusting in your relationship.

• 110–132: You are prone to jealousy, but it doesn't get in the way too often.

• 133 or higher: You are feeling pretty jealous. Think about the basis of your feelings, thoughts, and behaviors. Has your partner given you a reason to be jealous? If so, you may want to work on this with your partner. If not, are there are strategies that you can find to curb your jealousy?

Whether your total jealousy score is high or low, you will want to examine your jealousy subscores—this is a feature most jealousy tests don't have. It turns out that some kinds of jealousy are better than other kinds of jealousy. Each subscore measures a particular kind of jealousy (jealous thoughts, jealous behaviors, and jealous feelings).

Indeed, in romantic relationships, jealousy isn't always associated with problems. In fact, often feelings of jealousy are positively associated with feelings of love and commitment. If your Subscore 3 is high, but Subscores 1 and 2 are low, then your jealousy is not a problem, unless, of course, your feelings of jealousy bother your mate.

The second set of questions is about how people express their jealousy through their actions. Thus, if your Subscore 2 is high, then you may be doing things that are going to produce problems between you and your mate. Generally, higher scores on jealous *behaviors* were not associated with love at all. Subscore 1, regarding jealous thoughts, is also "negatively" associated with love. That is, studies find that the higher Subscore 1 was for research subjects, the lower was their love score.

From Susan Pfeiffer and Paul Wong, "Multidimensional Jealousy," *Journal of Social and Personal Relationships* 6 (1989): 181–96. Copyright © 1989 Sage Ltd. Reprinted by permission of the authors and Sage.

SELF-DISCLOSURE INVENTORY

This self-disclosure test measures your willingness to talk about the most personal things about yourself. Self-disclosure turns out to be a very strong correlate with love, intimacy, and longevity of relationships. Distancing, on the other hand, is associated with deteriorating relationships.

Directions: Read through each item. Based on the response scale provided below, indicate the extent to which you have talked about the respective issue with your significant other. Record your answers in the box following each statement.

Response Scale

0   I have told my significant other nothing about this aspect of me. Or I have lied or misrepre-

sented myself to the other person so that s/he has a false picture of me.

1 I have talked in general terms about this item, but my significant other has only a general idea about this aspect of me.

2 I have talked in full and complete detail about this item to my significant other. S/he knows me fully in this respect and could describe me accurately.

A. Attitudes and Opinions

1. What I think and feel about religion.   _____
2. My views on the present government.   _____
3. My personal views on sexual morality.   _____

Subscore A: _____

B. Tastes and Interests

4. My favorite foods, the ways I like food prepared, and my food dislikes.   _____
5. My likes and dislikes in music.   _____
6. The kind of party or social gathering that I like best, and the kind that I wouldn't enjoy.   _____

Subscore B: _____

C. Work

7. What I find to be the most boring and unenjoyable aspects of my work.   _____
8. What I enjoy most and get the most satisfaction from in my present work.   _____

9. What I feel are my shortcomings and hand-icaps that prevent me from getting further ahead in my work. _____

10. What I feel are my special strong points and qualifications for my work. _____

11. How I really feel about the people that I work for or with. _____

Subscore C: _____

D. Money

12. How much money I make at my work or receive from other sources. _____

13. Whether or not I owe money; if so, how much. _____

Subscore D: _____

E. Personality

14. The aspects of my personality that I dislike. _____

15. Whether or not I feel that I am sexually attractive. _____

16. Things in the past or present that I feel ashamed and guilty about. _____

17. The kinds of things that make me just furious. _____

18. What it takes to get me feeling really depressed or blue. _____

19. What it takes to get me really worried, anxious, and afraid. _____

20. What it takes to hurt my feelings deeply. _____

21. The kinds of things that make me especially proud of myself, elated, full of self-esteem or self-respect. _____

Subscore E: _____

F. Body

22. My feelings about the appearance of my face—things I don't like, and things that I might like about my face. _____

23. How I wish I looked. _____

24. My past record of illness and treatment. _____

25. Whether or not I now make a special effort to keep fit, healthy, and attractive. _____

Subscore F: _____

Scoring and Evaluaton

Create your subscores by adding together your responses in each of the six subsections of the test. Your total score is the sum of all six subscores. Record all your scores on the table below.

Meaning	Range	Scores
A. Attitudes and Opinions	0–6	_____
B. Tastes and Interests	0–6	_____
C. Work	0–10	_____
D. Money	0–4	_____
E. Personality	0–16	_____
F. Body	0–8	_____
Total	0–50	_____

If your total score is not particularly high, say, below 18, then chances are you are not staying particularly connected in your relationship, and you may want to work to create bridges and connections with your partner.

Higher subscores indicate areas in which you are more comfortable sharing with your partner. If your score is less than half of the highest possible score, in any category, this may be an area where you should focus your efforts to improve your relationship.

Although all six areas are important, the *Personality* score (E) might merit your particular attention, since this set of questions taps the kind of intimate knowledge that really helps lovers stay together.

Based on questions included in S. M. Jourard and P. Laskarow, "Some Factors in Self-Disclosure," *Journal of Abnormal and Social Psychology* 56 (1958): 91–98.

RELATIONSHIP DISCLOSURE TEST

The previous test, the Self-Disclosure Inventory, measured how much you share *about yourself* with your partner. By contast, The Relationship Disclosure Test focuses on how much you share *about things that may influence your relationship* with your partner. Research shows that couples can talk a blue streak but still not get into the really difficult and relationship-focused issues that may be important for the happiness and longevity of their relationship.

Directions: Use the scale below to indicate how likely it is that you would discuss each issue with your partner, and fill in the number in the appropriate column. Mark other relevant columns, also, if there are other individuals whom you would discuss the issue with.

9	8	7	6	5	4	3	2	1
extremely likely		somewhat likely		not very likely			not at all likely	

Relationship Disclosure	Would discuss with partner	Does not apply (mark X)	Would discuss with a friend?	Would discuss with a parent?	Would discuss with a relative?
1. Having trouble with your work.					
2. Being physically attracted to someone other than your partner.					
3. Beginning to fall in love with someone other than your partner.					
4. Important things about your partner that bother you.					

Relationship Disclosure	Would discuss with partner	Does not apply (mark X)	Would discuss with a friend?	Would discuss with a parent?	Would discuss with a relative?
5. Suspicions that your partner has been sexually unfaithful.					
6. Serious reservations about your relationship with your partner.					
7. Concerns about money.					
8. A health-related concern about your partner.					
9. A health-related problem of yours.					

Relationship Disclosure	Would discuss with partner	Does not apply (mark X)	Would discuss with a friend?	Would discuss with a parent?	Would discuss with a relative?
10. Any negative feelings you have about your partner's friends or family.					
11. Having sex with someone other than your partner.					
12. Qualities of yourself that you are ashamed of.					
13. How much you enjoy sex with your partner.					
Totals:					

Scoring and Evaluation

For this test, thinking about how you responded to each individual question is as valuable as getting an overview of how open you feel you can be about a troubling or difficult topic with your partner. To get an overall openness score, add your responses in the first column (Likelihood you'd discuss this) and divide by the number of questions you answered. (That is, all the questions for which you did *not* mark X in the second column [Does not apply].) Your score should be between 1 and 9.

Column 1 score: _____ ÷ number of relevant questions: _____ = Openness Score: _____

The higher your openness score, the more easily you are able to communicate with your partner.

• Scores between 7 and 9 are strong signs of disclosure in your relationship.

• Scores 3 or below indicate that there are a number of different areas where you keep your partner in the dark.

As the questions probably suggested to you, some of these issues are risky to raise in a close relationship. Willingness to take risks by being extremely honest is a sign of a strong relationship, but it is also a sign of your own self-confidence and autonomy.

The "talks to others" scores (third, fourth, and fifth columns) mean different things depending upon your openness score.

• With an openness score of 7 or higher, the more people you talk to about your issues, the more you have support from others in your circle. Social support like this is a valuable asset that helps good relationships stay strong and stable.

• If you have a high openness score, but you *don't talk to others*, your relationship is your private world. You may experience it as a private oasis where you share even the most difficult topics and prefer not to let anyone else in on your joys and troubles.

• If your openness score is 3 or lower and yet you talk to a number of other people about your issues, there's good news and bad news. The good news is that you're garnering support from the outside, and support is a key for healthy individuals as well as healthy relationships. The bad news is that you are leaving your partner out of the loop, and this may undermine the long-term stability of your relationship.

• If your openness score is 3 or lower, and you don't have anyone to talk to, this may be a very uncomfortable situation for you. With a confidante neither at home nor among your families and friends, you may be quite isolated.

Based on Philip Blumstein and Pepper Schwartz, *American Couples: Money, Work, and Sex* (New York: William Morrow, 1983). Updated by Virginia Rutter and Pepper Schwartz (1997).

ABBREVIATED RELATIONSHIP STANDARDS INVENTORY

This is a test of four different kinds of standards that you may or may not have for your relationship: boundaries, control, effort, and expression. The questionnaire was developed by leading couples researchers and therapists who are trying to discover why couples who start out happy can end up so unhappy.

Directions: This questionnaire asks about your standards for your relationship, or what you think your relationship *should be* like. The way you think your relationship should be might be different from the way your relationship actually is. Below are sixteen statements that describe standards that people may hold about their relationships.

For each question, there are three responses we'd like you to make.

Following each statement indicate in the *first column* how often you think you and your partner should act toward each other in the ways described in the statements. Your choices are:

5	4	3	2	1
always	usually	sometimes	seldom	never

In the *second column* circle Y if you are satisfied with the way that the standard is being met in your relationship, and circle N if you are not satisfied.

In the *third column*, use the following scale to indicate how upsetting it is to you when this standard is not met in your relationship. Remember, even if you are satisfied with how well the standard is being met, you may have an idea of how upset you would get if that standard did not continue to be met.

1	2	3
not upsetting	somewhat upsetting	very upsetting

Relationship Standards	How often should this happen?	Are you satisfied with it now?	How upset do you get about this?
1. My partner and I should have the same ideas about the values we teach our children (or values in general).		Y N	
2. My partner and I should have the same ideas about how to spend our leisure time together.		Y N	
3. My partner and I should have the same ideas about how the housework should be done.		Y N	
4. My partner and I should value the same qualities in a friend.		Y N	
Boundaries Score (sum of 1–4): _____		# of "No" _____	_____

Relationship Standards	How often should this happen?	Are you satisfied with it now?	How upset do you get about this?
5. My partner and I should have equal say about when we discuss certain positive thoughts and feelings that we have about the relationship.		Y N	
6. My partner and I should have equal say about what kinds of leisure activities we do together.		Y N	
7. My partner and I should have equal say about whether we discuss certain negative thoughts and feelings that we have about our relationship.		Y N	
8. My partner and I should have equal say about the things we spend our money on.		Y N	
Control Score (sum of 5–8):	_____	# of "No" _____	_____

Relationship Standards	How often should this happen?	Are you satisfied with it now?	How upset do you get about this?
9. We should spend a lot of time and energy expressing physical affection for each other.		Y N	
10. Each of us should put a great deal of effort and energy into developing good relationships with our partner's friends.		Y N	
11. Each of us should stop what we are doing if the other person wants to discuss some positive thoughts and feelings.		Y N	
12. We should make our leisure and fun time together a high priority in our relationship.		Y N	
Effort Score (sum of 9–12): _____		**# of "No"** _____	_____

Relationship Standards	How often should this happen?	Are you satisfied with it now?	How upset do you get about this?
13. We should spend extra money we have for things we enjoy as a couple.		Y N	
14. My partner and I should try to make the other feel better when one of us has had a problem with the children.		Y N	
15. We should show our care and commitment to each other by getting together with our partner's family, even if we do not want to.		Y N	
16. My partner and I should show interest in each other's leisure activities, as a way of demonstrating that we care about each other.		Y N	
Expression Score (sum of 13–16): _____		**# of "No"** _____	_____

Scoring and Evaluation

Use the two tables that follow to keep track of your scores on this four-part test.

You can write your scores in the Summary of Scores for Relationship Standards table to keep track of them. This will help you use the Global Score Table.

• To obtain your score for *Boundaries*, add up the answers to the first four questions in Column 1; do the same for Columns 2 and 3. For Column 2, you should give yourself a score of zero if you answered yes (Y) and a score of 1 if you answered no (N).

• For *Control*: Follow the same instructions for the next four questions.

• For *Effort*: Follow the same instructions for the next four questions.

• For *Expression*: Follow the same instructions for the next four questions.

• You can also create a sum of all scores in order to obtain a *Global Relationship* focused score.

• After creating your Global scores, select whether the score in each column is *high*, *medium*, or *low*. Here's how:

Column 1: If you have a score above 61 give yourself an H; if it is above 23 give yourself an M; 23 or below, give yourself an L. High scores are an indication of high standards.

Column 2: If you have a score above 12, give yourself an H; if it is above 4, give yourself an M; 4 or lower, give yourself an L.

Column 3: If you have a score above 40, give yourself an H. Above 24, give yourself an M; 24 or lower, give yourself an L.

SUMMARY OF SCORES FOR
RELATIONSHIP STANDARDS

Standard	Column 1 My standards	Column 2 My satisfaction	Column 3 How upset I am if standard is not met
Boundaries			
Control			
Effort			
Expression			
Global Score (sum of column):			
Range	*(4–80)*	*(0–16)*	*(14–48)*

Are you *high*, *medium*, or *low*	H M L	H M L	H M L

Interpreting your scores: This test actually evaluates four different kinds of standards.

Personal *boundaries*, or the extent to which you prefer intense closeness with your partner. Higher scores indicate a preference for intense closeness in a relationship.

Control or the extent to which you prefer to have significant influence over each conversation you have or decision you make as a couple. Higher control scores mean that you prefer to be involved and influential over every issue and decision related to your lives together.

Amount of *effort* you think is valuable for your life as a couple. Higher scores are related to high standards for shared activities that are dedicated to your relationship.

Expression means your standards for investing in pleasure and enjoyment as a couple. Higher scores mean you have a high standard for investing your joint resources in having fun and positive experiences together.

For each relationship standard the score under "My standards" is an indication of how important this area is to you. The range is from 1 to 20. The higher your score, the more important this area of the relationship is.

Next, your score under "My satisfaction" is an indication of whether you are satisfied with the way this standard is met. For each standard your score can range from 0 to 4. If your score is higher than 2 in any standard, then this is an area you may want to address with your partner.

Finally, the score under "How upset I am if standard is not met" indicates how emotional you are about these standards. The range is from 4 to 12 for each subscore, and a higher score is another indication of how crucial this standard is to your satisfaction and comfort in your relationship.

You may want to look at the table of scores in another way: For those standards where your "satisfaction" score is low but your "upset" score is high, there is little to worry about in this area, since your needs related to that standard are being met. But for those standards where your "satisfaction" score is high and your "upset" score is high, these issues should probably take a high priority for working on your relationship.

To evaluate the global score, there are several considerations. You can use the global scores in columns 1 and 3 to evaluate how relationship-focused you are. For column 1, the range is from 4 to 80. Higher scores in column 1 reflect how relationship-focused you are. You have a lot of standards for what an ideal relationship should be like. This is neither good nor bad, but a description. What matters is whether those standards are being met or not.

Global Score Table. Use the Global Score Table on page 98 to figure out how your standards affect your relationship satisfaction. To use this table, match your responses in the last row (H, M, or L) of the Summary of Scores for Relationship Standards Table to its twin in the Global Score Table to learn what the pattern in your responses mean.

GLOBAL SCORE TABLE

Standard	Dissatisfaction with standard	How upset I am if standard is not met	What this means
H	H	H	The reality of your relationship doesn't live up to your standards, and this is upsetting.
H	H	L	Your relationship is not meeting your standards, but you aren't getting upset about it.
H	L or M	L or M	You have a strong sense of how your relationship should be, and your relationship is meeting your standards.
L or M	L or M	L or M	You have a strong sense of your relationship and are very relaxed about your own situation.

These questions were taken from the Inventory of Specific Relationship Standards, developed by Don Baucom, Norman Epstein, Lynn Rankin, and Charles Burnett, 1993. Baucom is professor of psychology and director of clinical training at the University of North Carolina–Chapel Hill. Reprinted by permission of the authors.

COMMUNICATION
PATTERNS
QUESTIONNAIRE

This test not only evaluates your constructive communication patterns; it also gives you information about whether you and your partner engage in what is called the *demand/withdraw* pattern (also called the *pursuer-distancer* pattern).

"Demand/withdraw" is a pattern where one partner seeks closeness (i.e., s/he is demanding or pursuing) and the other partner responds, almost automatically, by withdrawing and seeking distance.

The demand/withdraw pattern can be very destructive for couples; and what is so frustrating about demand/withdraw is that when one partner starts, by demanding or withdrawing, it is very difficult to resist reacting in a withdrawing or a demanding way. Some therapists call it a "mutual trap" because both partners are stuck in a pattern that is very hard to stop.

Directions: Rate each item on a scale of 1 to 9 (displayed below) in terms of how you and your partner typically deal with problems in your relationship. Record your responses in the boxes provided.

9   8   7   6   5   4   3   2   1
very likely   very unlikely

A. When some problem in the relationship arises:
 1. Both partners avoid discussing the problem.   ____
 2. Both partners try to discuss the problem.   ____
3a. I try to start a discussion while my
    partner tries to avoid it.   ____
3b. My partner tries to start a discussion
    while I try to avoid it.

 B. During a discussion of a relationship problem:
 1. Both members blame, accuse, and criticize
    each other.   ____
 2. Both partners express their feelings to each
    other.   ____
 3. Both partners threaten each other with
    negative consequences.   ____
 4. Both partners suggest possible solutions and
    compromises.   ____
5a. I nag and make demands while my partner
    withdraws, becomes silent, or refuses to
    discuss the matter further.   ____

5b. My partner nags and makes demands
while I withdraw, become silent, or
refuse to discuss the matter further.   ___

6a. I criticize while my partner defends him/
herself.   ___

6b. My partner criticizes while I defend
myself.   ___

7a. I pressure my partner to take some action
or stop some action, while my partner
resists.   ___

7b. My partner pressures me to take some
action or stop some action, while I resist.   ___

8a. I express my feelings while my partner
offers reasons and solutions.   ___

8b. My partner expresses feelings while I offer
reasons and solutions.   ___

9a. I threaten negative consequences and my
partner gives in or backs down.   ___

9b. My partner threatens negative
consequences and I give in or back down.   ___

10a. I call my partner names, swear at him/
her, or attack his/her character.   ___

10b. My partner calls me names, swears at
me, or attacks my character.   ___

11a. I push, shove, slap, hit, or kick my
partner.   ___

11b. My partner pushes, shoves, slaps, hits, or
kicks me.   ___

C. After a discussion of a relationship problem:

1. We each feel the other has understood our position. ___

2. We both withdraw from each other after the discussion. ___

3. We both feel that the problem has been solved. ___

4. Neither of us is giving (or generous) to the other after the discussion. ___

5. We both try to be especially nice to each other. ___

6a. I feel guilty for what I said or did while my partner feels hurt. ___

6b. My partner feels guilty for what s/he said or did while I feel hurt. ___

7a. I try to be especially nice, act as if things are back to normal, and my partner acts distant. ___

7b. My partner tries to be especially nice, act as if things are back to normal, and I act distant. ___

8a. I pressure my partner to apologize or promise to do better, while my partner resists. ___

8b. My partner pressures me to apologize or promise to do better, while I resist. ___

9a. I seek support from others (parent, friend, children). ___

9b. My partner seeks support from others (parent, friend, children). ___

Scoring and Evaluation

Mutual Constructive Communication Score: Calculate the scores as follows:

(A2 + B2 + B4) minus (B1 + B3 + 10A + 10B). The range of answers is from −24 to +24.

That's right, you can have a negative number as a score. The score is the sum of "positive communication styles" minus the sum of "negative communication styles." As you can imagine, people need to have more positive communication than negative communication to be happy. If your score is above zero, then you are doing well. If your score is zero or below, the research indicates that this may signal problems in communication that are leading your relationship into distressed territory. This doesn't prove that your relationship is on the rocks by any means, but it does tell you that your communication styles are a problem.

• *Demand/Withdraw Communication Scores*: How much demand/withdraw communication is there in your relationship?

To get this total, add together A3a + A3b+ B5a +B5b +B6a+B6b.

The higher this score is, the more common the demander/withdrawer pattern is in your relationship. The range is from 6 to 54. A score above 30 suggests this pattern is an issue in your relationship, according to our evaluation of the research.

Are you the demander or the withdrawer?

• To get your demander score, add together A3a+ B5a +B6a. The range for this score is from 3 to 27. If you scored above 18, then you may be the demander in the couple (which means your partner may be a withdrawer).

• To get your withdrawer score, add together A3b+ B5b+B6b. The range for this score is from 3 to 27. Again, if you scored above 18, then you may be the withdrawer, and your partner may be a demander.

Although the demand/withdraw pattern can be difficult to overcome, it can be surmounted, in part, by recognizing it as a couple problem and not one person's fault. Christensen and colleague Neil Jacobson call this "turning the problem into an it."

One of the interesting things in the research on demand/withdraw patterns has to do with gender. The stereotype is that women are demanders, nagging for this or that, while men are the withdrawers, staying silent and ignoring "her" pleas. It turns out, however, that this is not always the case. True, in research by UCLA Psychology Professor Andrew Christensen and others, women tend to be demanders more often, and men withdrawers. However, Christensen notes, depending upon the problem, the reverse pattern occurs (where women are withdrawers and men are demanders) about one-third of the time. About 10% of the time, both patterns occurred.

Finally, there is one additional score that you can draw from the CPQ:

• *The Mutual Avoidance and Withholding Score* can be calculated by adding together A1+C2+C4. The range for this score is from 3 to 27. High scores on this one, above 18, are cause for concern. In research by numerous psychological scientists, the avoidance and withholding stance in relationships is a sign of serious problems that require your attention. Mutual avoidance means that both partners withdraw whenever there is conflict. Even happy couples may be uncomfortable with conflict and use this strategy to avoid conflict. But over time this pattern can lead to distancing and leading "parallel lives" where there is no shared emotional life between the partners.

Other questions to which you responded are not included in the scoring above. They also reveal information about how partners interact with each other. Blame, pressure, aggression, and guilt induction are other things you or your partner can do that will make matters worse, not better. You can detect these by looking at your responses to questions B1, 7a and 7b and 8a and 8b, and 10a and 10b and 11a and 11b. Higher scores on these questions suggest that you and your partner try to manipulate each other in conflicts. Often these strategies are used to gain power.

On the other hand, "making nice," and even seeking outside support are constructive activities following conflict, as indicated in questions 5, 9a, and 9b. Higher scores on these questions suggest that you are managing your conflicts well—which is important to sustaining a happy relationship.

Based on the Communication Patterns Questionnaire by A. Christensen and Megan Sulloway, as reported in: Andrew Christensen and C. L. Heavy, "Gender Differences in Marital Conflict: The Demand-Withdraw Interaction Pattern" in *Gender Issues in Contemporary Society,* ed. S. Oskamp and M. Costanzo (Newbury Park: Sage, 1993). Researchers who wish to use the CPQ should contact Prof. Christensen at UCLA Department of Psychology, Los Angeles, CA 90095. Reprinted by permission of the authors.

SEX WITH SOMEONE YOU LOVE

IN THIS SECTION YOU WILL LEARN: HOW UP-
TO-DATE YOU ARE WHEN IT COMES TO SEX
AND SEXUAL ACTIVITY • WHAT YOUR SEXUAL
ATTITUDES ARE • HOW SEXUALLY SATISFIED
YOU AND YOUR PARTNER ARE • HOW HAPPY
AND COMFORTABLE YOU ARE WITH THE WAY
YOU TALK TO EACH OTHER ABOUT
SEX • WHAT YOUR ATTITUDES AND VULNERA-
BILITY TOWARD AFFAIRS ARE • WHETHER YOU
ARE HAVING AN "EMOTIONAL AFFAIR"

THE KINSEY INSTITUTE NEW REPORT ON SEX QUIZ

While this test isn't specifically about your relationship, we thought that a section on sex ought to help you assess what you know and don't know about sex, since knowledge is pretty important for sexual satisfaction and ease in communication. When the following test was given to a representative sample of Americans in 1990, the vast majority failed it. Women did better than men, and younger people did better than folks over forty-five.

Directions: Circle one answer after reading each question carefully.

1. Nowadays, what do you think is the age at which the *average* or *typical* American first has sexual intercourse?

a. 11 or younger	e. 15	i. 19
b. 12	f. 16	j. 20
c. 13	g. 17	k. 21 or older
d. 14	h. 18	l. don't know

2. Out of every ten married American men, how many would you estimate have had an extramarital affair—that is, have been sexually unfaithful to their wives?

a. Less than 1 out of 10.	e. 40%	j. 90%
b. One out of 10 (10%)	f. 50%	k. More than 90%
	g. 60%	l. don't know
	h. 70%	
c. 20%	i. 80%	
d. 30%		

3. Out of every ten American women, how many would you estimate have had anal (rectal) intercourse?

a. Less than 1 out of 10.	d. 30%	i. 80%
b. One out of 10 (10%)	e. 40%	j. 90%
	f. 50%	k. More than 90%
	g. 60%	l. don't know
c. 20%	h. 70%	

4. A person can get AIDS by having anal intercourse even if neither partner is infected with the AIDS virus.

a. true   b. false   c. don't know

5. Petroleum jelly, Vaseline Intensive Care, baby oil, and Nivea are *not* good lubricants to use with a condom or diaphragm.

   a. true   b. false   c. don't know

6. More than one out of four American men have had a sexual experience with another male during either their teens or adult years.

   a. true   b. false   c. don't know

7. It is usually difficult to tell whether people *are* or *are not* homosexual just by their appearance or gestures.

   a. true   b. false   c. don't know

8. A woman or teenage girl can get pregnant during her menstrual flow (her "period").

   a. true   b. false   c. don't know

9. A woman or teenage girl can get pregnant even if the man withdraws his penis before he ejaculates (before he "comes").

   a. true   b. false   c. don't know

10. Unless they are having sex, women do not need to have regular gynecological examinations.

   a. true   b. false   c. don't know

11. Teenage boys (and men) should examine their testicles ("balls") regularly just as women self-examine their breasts for lumps.

    a. true   b. false   c. don't know

12. Problems with erection are most often started by a physical condition.

    a. true   b. false   c. don't know

13. Almost all erection problems can be successfully treated.

    a. true   b. false   c. don't know

14. Menopause, or change of life as it is often called, does *not* cause most women to lose interest in having sex.

    a. true   b. false   c. don't know

15. Out of every ten American women, how many would you estimate have masturbated either as children or after they have grown up?

    a. Less than 1   d. 30%   i. 80%
       out of 10   e. 40%   j. 90%
    b. One out of   f. 50%   k. More than 90%
       10 (10%)   g. 60%   l. don't know
    c. 20%   h. 70%

16. What do you think is the length of the average man's *erect* penis?

a. 2 inches   e. 6 inches   i. 10 inches
b. 3 inches   f. 7 inches   j. 11 inches
c. 4 inches   g. 8 inches   k. 12 inches
d. 5 inches   h. 9 inches   l. don't know

17. Most women prefer a sexual partner with a larger-than-average penis.

a. true   b. false   c. don't know

Scoring and Evaluation
Using the following answer key, give yourself one point for each correct answer.

Answer key: 1 - f or g; 2- d or e; 3- d or e; 4 -b. false; 5 - a. true; 6 - a. true; 7 - a. true; 8 - a. true; 9 - a. true; 10 - b. false; 11 - a. true; 12 - a. true; 13 - a. true; 14 - a. true; 15 - g, h, or i; 16 - d, e, or f; 17 - b. false.

Grading:
A 16–17   C 12–13   F 1–9
B 14–15   D 10–11

The more correct answers you made, the higher your "Sex I.Q." What is important, especially when it comes to issues of sexual functioning, contraception, and sexual health, is that you and your partner know the facts. And remember to use what you know so that you don't run into problems or disagreements about the variety of practical issues related to sex.

For your information and amusement, we have included abridged comments from *The Kinsey Institute New Report on Sex* relative to the questions:

1. Knowing that the age of first sex isn't as young as many people think can help people avoid peer pressure into sex they don't really want.
2. It turns out that not as many men have affairs as everyone thinks.
3. Heterosexuals, not just gay men, try anal sex more than most people assume.
4. It isn't anal sex, but penetration with an HIV-infected partner, that makes infection more likely.
5. Petroleum-based products make microscopic holes in condoms and diaphragms large enough for HIV to pass through.
6. Many more men have had at least one sexual encounter with another man than is generally thought to be true.
7. The majority of Americans got this one right—gays, lesbians, and heterosexuals have a variety of appearances.
8. During a woman's period, she is less likely to get pregnant than at other times, but it is possible.
9. Before ejaculation, some seminal fluid is released and can therefore lead to pregnancy.
10. All women should have annual gynecological examinations after the age of eighteen.

11. Beginning at puberty, men should check their testicles monthly for lumps or changes.

12. While physical dysfunction or alcohol or drug use often initiate erectile problems, men can also get "psyched out" and can be helped by counseling.

13. Yes, erection problems are highly treatable.

14. Most people over fifty—both men and women—continue to have active and healthy sex lives.

15. At least 60 to 80 percent of adult women have tried masturbation.

16. Those people who answered incorrectly were twice as likely to *overestimate* penis length.

17. Men worry about penis size more than women. According to the research, most women don't usually express a preference for size.

From June Reinisch, Ph.D., with Ruth Beasley, M.L.S. *The Kinsey Institute New Report on Sex: What You Must Know to Be Sexually Literate*, copyright © 1990 by Kinsey Institute for Research in Sex, Gender and Reproduction. Reprinted by permission of St. Martin's Press, Inc.

SEXUAL ATTITUDES TEST

While sex is a very personal issue, sexual issues are sometimes quite political. This test helps you examine your attitudes toward sexual activity in your own life—as well as in general. It is an opportunity to explore your partner's attitudes, too.

Directions: Indicate how strongly you agree or disagree with the items listed below. A space is provided for your partner to take this test also.

1	2	3	4	5	6	7	8	9
strongly agree				**neither agree nor disagree**				**strongly disagree**

Sexual Attitude	Your Attitude	Partner's Attitude
1. The law has no business regulating sexual relations between consenting adults.*		
2. There should be stronger laws against selling erotic reading material.*		
3. As long as it doesn't include child pornography, sex on the internet is fine.		
4. Consenting adults should feel free to engage in group sex, S & M, role-playing or any other sexual activity.		
5. Sex education should not be taught in the schools.*		
6. Prostitutes and their customers should be subject to fines and imprisonment.*		

Sexual Attitude	Your Attitude	Partner's Attitude
7. If two people like each other, there is nothing wrong with having sexual relations.		
8. Sex with someone other than one's partner is wrong under any circumstances.		
9. A woman who has many sexual partners before marriage is probably not well adjusted.*		
10. Gay men and lesbians should feel free to hold hands in public if they want to.		
11. Gay men and lesbians are entitled to legally sanctioned commitments or marriage.		
12. Abortion may not be the choice for everybody, but it is a private choice, and women are entitled to it.		
Totals (See reverse scoring* instructions before completing)	_____	_____

Scoring and Evaluation

Before you add together all of your responses, reverse-score items 1, 2, 5, 6, 9. To "reverse score" subtract your response from 10. (If you responded 2, for example, then your answer is 10 minus 2, or 8.) Then add together all your responses. The total should range between 12 and 108.

The higher your scores, the more conservative you are when it comes to sexual issues; the lower your scores, the more liberal you are when it comes to sexual issues. Below is a continuum where you can locate yourself:

12	20	30	40	50	60	70	80	100	108
sexually		liberal		moderate		conservative			arch
progres-									conserv-
sive									ative

"sex positive"   " sex negative"

If you are on the left side of the continuum, then you are "sex positive": you believe in diversity of sexual expression, and you tend to view pleasure as an important component of sexual expression. If your score falls to the right side of the continuum, then you tend to view sexuality as something that is primarily for a married couple to share with each other exclusively.

In research this questionnaire is based on, Philip Blumstein and Pepper Schwartz found that married people are more conservative than people who are single or cohabiting; and married men are more conservative than married women. However, there are no norms or standards for responses to this questionnaire.

It is useful, however, to examine how *different* you and your partner are on sexuality attitudes. Partners can disagree on political issues, and even sexuality issues. This questionnaire raises questions, however, that might not otherwise come up until you are surprised by your partner's views—or your own.

Based on Philip Blumstein and Pepper Schwartz, *American Couples: Money, Work, and Sex*, 1983. Questionnaire revised by Virginia Rutter and Pepper Schwartz, 1997.

SEXUAL INTERACTION AND SATISFACTION SCALE

The sexual interaction inventory helps evaluate how satisfied you are with the *variety of things you and your partner do together* when you have sex. (This is different from evaluating how satisfied you are with sexual frequency—a question that comes up in other tests in this book.)

Directions: Below is a list of sexual activities followed by two columns for responses. In the first column you should provide the number, corresponding with the scale provided below, which describes what percentage of the time each activity happens when you are intimate. In the second column you should provide the number, also corresponding with the scale below, which describes how often you wish this would happen when you have sex. In the third column, record the differences of the two numbers.

(See scoring instructions following the inventory before completing this column.)

Possible responses:
 6 Always
 5 Usually (75% of the time)
 4 Fairly often (50% of the time)
 3 Occasionally (25% of the time)
 2 Rarely (10% of the time)
 1 Never

Sexual Activity	How often does this happen?	How often would you like it to happen?	What's the difference?
1. Seeing your partner nude.			
2. Your partner seeing you nude.			
3. Kissing together for one minute continuously.			
4. Giving your partner a body massage without touching sexual parts.			
5. Your partner giving you a body massage without touching your sexual parts.			

Sexual Activity	How often does this happen?	How often would you like it to happen?	What's the difference?
6. Caressing your partner's private parts with your hands.			
7. Your partner caressing your private parts with his/her hands.			
8. Caressing your partner's private parts with your lips or mouth.			
9. Your partner caressing your private parts with his/her lips or mouth.			
10. Caressing your partner until s/he reaches orgasm.			
11. Your partner caressing you until you reach orgasm.			
12. Having sexual intercourse.			

Sexual Activity	How often does this happen?	How often would you like it to happen?	What's the difference?
13. Having sexual intercourse until both of you have an orgasm.			
Total (sum of column)	_____	_____	_____

Scoring and Evaluation

Based on our evaluation of the research, we suggest the following scoring system. To score this test fill in the third ("What's the difference?") column for each of the thirteen items with the number that represents the difference between column 1 and column 2. To obtain this number, subtract the smaller of the two numbers from the larger of the two numbers. So, for example, if your answer on question 1, column 1 is 5 and your answer on question 1, column 2 is 6, the difference is 6–5, or 1.

Once you have calculated the difference scores for each of the 13 items, then you should create a sum of the difference scores. Below is a guide for interpreting your total difference score.

• A score below 13 means that you are quite happy with your sex life as it is.

• A score between 13 and 31 means that you and your partner are nearly on the same page when it comes to having sex.

• A score from 32 to 39 suggests that you are interested in change.

• A score above 40 suggests that you aren't doing what you want sexually much of the time and there may be a few areas where you are very much interested in change.

• A score of 52 or higher suggests that you are very dissatisfied, indeed.

Use this test with your partner as a way to raise some of the issues with him/her—or to confirm how well you are doing. If it seems as though talking about these aspects of your sex life would be awkward, you may also want to take a look at the next questionnaire, Sexual Communication Satisfaction Scale, which covers talking about sex.

Based on the Sexual Interaction Inventory, created by University of Missouri Professor of Psychology Joseph LoPiccolo. LoPiccolo is the author, with Julia Heiman, of *Becoming Orgasmic: A Personal and Sexual Growth Program for Women* (1988). Reprinted by permission of the author.

Sexual Communication Satisfaction Scale

Sexual communication is more difficult for some people than others. It involves talking about sex, but it also involves actions that help partners understand what is appealing and unappealing in bed. Even people with good relationships in other areas may find communicating about sex a particularly difficult area, because there are many taboos against sexual expression. Plus, this isn't something most people get to practice at a whole lot!

Couples who can communicate well about their sex lives can gain more closeness in general as well as more pleasure in bed, so it is worth the effort to try to keep each other informed about the experience.

Directions: Please respond to the questions using the following scale of responses to indicate how strongly you agree or disagree with each statement.

1	2	3	4	5
strongly agree	agree	neutral	disagree	strongly disagree

Statements About Communication

Agree or dis- agree?

1. I tell my partner when I am especially sexually satisfied.   _____

2. I am satisfied with my partner's ability to communicate his/her sexual desires to me.   _____

3. I do not let my partner know things that I find pleasing during sex.   _____

4. I am very satisfied with the quality of our sexual interactions.   _____

5. I do not hesitate to let my partner know when I want to have sex.   _____

6. I do not tell my partner whether or not I am sexually satisfied.   _____

7. I am dissatisfied over the degree to which my partner and I discuss our sexual relationship.   _____

8. I am not afraid to show my partner what kind of sexual behavior I find satisfying.   _____

9. I am displeased with the manner in which my partner and I communicate with each other during sex.   _____

10. My partner does not show me when s/he is sexually satisfied.   _____

11. I show my partner what pleases me during
sex.   _____

12. I am displeased with the manner in which my
partner and I communicate with each other
during sex.   _____

13. My partner does not show me things s/he
finds pleasing during sex.   _____

14. I show my partner when I am sexually
satisfied.   _____

15. My partner does not let me know whether
sex has been satisfying or not.   _____

16. I do not show my partner when I am
sexually satisfied.   _____

17. I am satisfied concerning my ability to communicate about sexual matters with my partner.   _____

18. My partner shows me by the ways s/he
touches me if s/he is satisfied.   _____

19. I am dissatisfied with my partner's ability to
communicate his/her sexual desire to me.   _____

20. I have no way of knowing when my partner
is sexually satisfied.   _____

21. I am not satisfied in the majority of our
sexual interactions.   _____

22. I am pleased with the manner in which my
partner and I communicate with each other
after sex.   _____

**Sexual Communication
Satisfaction Total
[range: 22–110]:**   _____

Scoring and Evaluation

First, reverse score statements 1, 2, 4, 5, 8, 11, 14, 17, 18, and 22. To reverse score, subtract your response from 6. Then add up all your responses for your total sexual communication satisfaction score. The higher your score is, the more satisfied you are with your sexual communication. Use our guide below to understand your scores in greater detail.

- 100–110: Congratulations, and keep up the good work!
- 66–99: This is a good score. Your sexual communication is high functioning.
- 44–65: If you scored in this range, you may want to try to identify the particular areas about which it is hard for you to communicate, and look for ways to become more comfortable with talking about these items.
- 43 or lower: Sexual communication is an area that needs your attention.

Based on: Lawrence Wheeles, Virginia Wheeles, and Raymond Baus, "Sexual Communication, Communication Satisfaction and Solidarity in the Developmental Stages of Intimate Relationships," *Western Journal of Speech Communication* 48 (1984): p. 224. Reprinted by permission of the Western Speech Communication Association. Copyright © 1984 WSCA.

JUSTIFICATIONS FOR EXTRAMARITAL INVOLVEMENT QUESTIONNAIRE

Being married doesn't preclude anyone from being involved in relationships with friends or acquaintances of the opposite sex. Of course, these relationships vary in degree of intimacy and may include emotional and/or sexual involvement. The following inventory lists reasons that people sometimes give to explain why they have been involved with someone of the opposite sex in a very close relationship outside their marriage.

Directions: Choose the response from the following list (and the number next to each item) to complete the sentence "I would feel _____ justified . . ." and indicate to what extent each of the following reasons would justify either an emotional or a sexual extramarital relationship for you.

1	2	3	4
completely unjustified	not justified	partially justified	completely justified

I would feel . . . justified having an extramarital relationship . . .

Reason   **Score**

1. For fun.(II)   ———
2. For intellectual sharing. (II)   ———
3. For a romantic experience.(I)   ———
4. To feel young.(V)   ———
5. To relieve sexual deprivation or frustration.
   (I)   ———
6. For someone to understand problems and
   feelings. (II)   ———
7. To enjoy sexual relations. (I)   ———
8. For sexual experimentation or curiosity. (I)   ———
9. For companionship. (II)   ———
10. For sexual excitement. (I)   ———
11. To get love and affection. (III)   ———
12. To enhance self-confidence and self-
    esteem. (V)   ———
13. For novelty and change. (I)   ———
14. To be respected. (V)   ———
15. Falling in love with another person. (III)   ———
16. To get even with a spouse. (IV)   ———
17. To advance in my career. (IV)   ———

Total: ———

Scoring and Evaluation

To understand your responses to this test, first add up the total score. Then you need to create five subscores that rate the four areas in which people sometimes feel justified or vulnerable to affairs. Add up the scores for the questions following by the respective Roman numerals I through V. Record these individual scores below:

Sexual: (sum of questions followed by I)_____   (range 6–24)

Social/Emotional: (sum of questions followed by II) _____(range 4–16)

Love: (sum of questions followed by III) _____ (range 2–8)

External Gain: (sum of questions IV) _____(range 2–8)

Ego-Building: (sum of questions V) _____(range 2–8)

Total (sum of all subscores) _____(range 17–68)

The lower your score is overall, the less vulnerable you are to having an affair.

About the subscores: Each subscore evaluates a different "vulnerability" area. The lower your subscore in a particular area, the less likely this is the kind of justification that would make you vulnerable to an affair.

Sexual: Higher scores on "sexual" mean that an affair that is for the purpose of having sex may seem justifiable to you. Men tend to be subject to this vulnerability more often than women, but (some of) both men and women experience this vulnerability.

Social/Emotional: Higher scores on "social/emotional"

suggest that affairs might be acceptable to you if the relationship satisfies a desire to be social and intimate.

Love: Higher scores on this measure appear among those people who would consider an affair if they were in love. While there are more women than men that show up as scoring higher on this measure, (some of) both women and men experience this vulnerability.

External Gain: External gain means that affairs are okay if you get some other benefit out of it. A person who scores high on extrinsic gain is a person who thinks that having an affair in order to gain some other external benefit beyond the affair itself is acceptable.

Ego-Building: Higher scores on ego-building suggest that a person would be prepared to get involved (or has gotten involved) in order to feel good about him or herself and build self-esteem.

As you can imagine, it is not possible to use these scores to predict who will or will not have an affair—or even who is in or has had an affair; thus, there are no "cut-points" that researchers and therapists use when they give this questionnaire to people.

Instead, this test is useful to help respondents (or psychologists) recognize the kinds of justifications that a particular person might use for him/herself. Research by psychologists Shirley Glass and Thomas Wright on this scale captured attention primarily because it demonstrated that while some people are more vulnerable to affairs than others, a larger proportion of people than expected do have reasons under which they think that an affair is justified, even though they may disapprove of other reasons for affairs.

EMOTIONAL AFFAIR QUESTIONNAIRE

Psychologist Dr. Shirley Glass established eight key questions to help you understand how much of a threat a special friendship you might have with someone other than your partner can be to your relationship. The following questionnaire helps you understand whether your partner's jealousy is justified. Answer yes or no to each of the following eight questions:

1. Do you confide more to your friend than your mate about how your day went?   Y or N
2. Do you discuss negative feelings or intimate details about your marriage with your friend?   Y or N
3. Are you open with your mate about the extent of your involvement with your friend?   Y or N

4. Would you feel comfortable if your mate
   heard your conversations with your friend?   Y or N
5. Would you feel comfortable if your mate
   saw a videotape of your meetings?   Y or N
6. Are you aware of sexual tensions in this
   friendship?   Y or N
7. Do you and your friend touch differently
   when you're alone than in front of others?   Y or N
8. Are you in love with your friend?   Y or N

Scoring and Evaluation

For each answer that is the same as the list below, give
   yourself one point.

1. Y	4. N	7. Y
2. Y	5. N	8. Y
3. N	6. Y	

Total: _____

If you scored zero or near zero, this sounds like a pla-
tonic friendship. A score of 7 to 8 is a danger sign for an
emotional affair because it involves emotional intimacy,
sexual chemistry, and secrecy from your significant other.

In her research, Dr. Glass learned that more and more
people are finding close connections with others at work
or other activities. Although the rates at which people have
extramarital affairs is difficult to obtain, a variety of
research has established that probably between 25 to 50
percent of married people have a (sexual) affair at some
time during the marriage. Glass is one of the few people

who has studied *emotional* affairs. In her study as many as 20 percent of the men and 24 percent of the women had at least a modestly strong emotional attachment to a friend who was not their spouse.

Questions based on Shirley P. Glass and Thomas L. Wright, "Justifications for Extramarital Relationships: The Association between Attitudes, Behaviors, and Gender," *Journal of Sex Research* 29 (1992): 361–87. Questions by Shirley Glass, Ph.D. Reprinted by permission of USA Today.

GETTING A FAIR DEAL

IN THIS SECTION YOU WILL LEARN: WHO
DOES WHAT AROUND THE HOUSE—AND HOW
YOU FEEL ABOUT IT • WHO REALLY DOES
WHAT WITH RESPECT TO INTIMACY • HOW
WELL YOU MANAGE MONEY TOGETHER • WHAT
YOUR PRIORITIES ARE FOR TIES TO YOUR
PARENTS—AND YOUR PARTNER'S
PARENTS • HOW MUCH YOU SACRIFICE YOUR
OWN FEELINGS FOR THE SAKE OF THE RELA-
TIONSHIP • WHETHER YOU BELIEVE IN TRADI-
TIONAL ROLES OR "EGALITARIANISM" IN
RELATIONSHIPS, AND WHAT IT MEANS FOR
YOUR RELATIONSHIP

WHO DOES
WHAT? QUIZ

All couples develop ways of dividing household tasks, decision making, and (if they are parents) the caring and rearing of children. This quiz, adapted from the Who Does What? (WDW?) Questionnaire, asks you to describe how *household* tasks are divided between you. This test was designed for married or cohabiting couples, but it may be interesting to use to look back at a previous relationship, or to help you to determine what your standards might be the next time you are in a relationship.

Directions: Please show how you and your partner divide the family tasks listed below. Using the numbers on the scale below, show how it is *now* in the first column, and how you *would like it to be* in the second column. The third column is to record the difference between the two.

Who Does What? Scale:

1	2	3	4	5	6	7	8	9
I do it all			We share equally			Partner does it all		

Household Task	How it is now	How I would like it to be	Satisfaction with Who Does What (difference between columns 1 and 2)
1. Planning and preparing meals			
2. Cleaning up after meals			
3. Repairs around the home			
4. House cleaning			
5. Taking out the garbage			
6. Buying groceries/ household needs			
7. Paying bills			

Household Task	How it is now	How I would like it to be	Satisfaction with Who Does What (difference between columns 1 and 2)
8. Laundry: washing, folding, ironing			
9. Writing letters, making calls to family/friends			
10. Looking after the car			
11. Providing income			
12. Caring for plants, garden, yard			
13. Working outside the family			
Total (sum of columns)	_____	_____	_____

Scoring and Evaluation

• To obtain your WDW? *current activities* score ("How it is now"), add up all the numbers in the first column of numbers.

• To obtain your WDW? *ideal activities* score ("How I would like it to be"), add up all the numbers in the second column of numbers.

- To obtain your *satisfaction with WDW?* score, calculate the difference between columns one and two for each item on the list, and record each "difference" in the third column entitled "Satisfaction with Who Does What."
- Then find the sum of those scores and fill them in on the Totals line at the bottom of the table.

The range for "How it is now" is from 13 to 127. The lower this score, the more you are carrying the load for you and your family. To interpret your scores, divide your total by 13. You should get a number that is between 1 and 9. Use the Who Does What? Scale above to locate yourself in terms of how, overall, you and your partner are sharing the work.

Use your "How I would like it to be" score to determine what your ideal "Who Does What" situation is. Divide your sum by 13. You should get a number between 1 and 9. You can locate your ideal level of sharing or dividing work on the Who Does What? Scale.

The range for "How I would like it to be" is also from 13 to 127. If the score for "How it is now" is lower than the score for "How I would like it to be," then you want your partner to do more of the work. If the score for "How I would like it to be" is lower than the score for "How it is now," then you feel you should do more of the work.

Finally, in the "Satisfaction with Who Does What" column, the lower your total score, the more satisfied you are with the distribution of labor in your relationship across each item. How many of the items involved a difference of 3 points or more? Differences above 3 points indicate that these are the areas where you might want to focus on creating change.

Psychologists and sociologists increasingly have been studying how partners share housework and domestic obligations. It turns out that it is perceptions and attitudes about housework that matter more than who actually does what in terms of how satisfied partners are in their relationship. In other words, you may be in a relationship where you do a lot more than your partner does (or vice versa). But the satisfaction score in column three is what matters most. Note that other research has demonstrated that the greater the burden of housework and child care that rests upon wives/mothers/women in relationships with men, the higher their odds of being depressed—and less satisfied with the relationship.

Finally, the importance of housework has been illustrated by some very interesting research by sociologist Julie Brines at the University of Washington. She has found that, in dual-earner married couples, wives who earn less than their husbands do more housework—this is a not very surprising exchange relationship. When wives earn about the same as their husbands, the couples tend to do about the same amount of housework. But in couples where wives earn more than their husbands, guess what? They actually also do more housework than their husbands do! Who does what is a very important issue in the lives of couples, but the ways in which it is important are surprising because they have to do with what men and women feel they ought to do to be good wives and husbands.

From the Who Does What? Questionnaire created by University of California at Berkeley psychologists Carolyn Pape Cowan and Philip Cowan, authors of *When Partners Become Parents* (1992). Selection reprinted by permission of the authors.

WHO DOES MORE?

This brief questionnaire evaluates how much you and your partner do in your relationship when it comes to some key aspects of well-functioning relationships.

Directions: For each of the key aspects of marriage listed below, circle the rating that best answers which spouse does more of the following:

Aspects of Marriage	I do more	We do about the same	Partner does more
1. Who enhances the other's self-confidence more?	A	B	C
2. Who tells more about how the day went?	A	B	C

Aspects of Marriage	I do more	We do about the same	Partner does more
3. Who does more romantic things?	A	B	C
4. Who understands the other's problems and feelings more?	A	B	C
5. Who respects the other more?	A	B	C
6. Who expresses more love and affection?	A	B	C
7. Who wants to have sexual relations more?	A	B	C
8. Who enjoys sexual relations more?	A	B	C
Total	# A's____	# B's____	# C's____

Scoring and Evaluation

Add up the number of responses you have in each column—
there's a possible range of from 1 to 8 for each column.

The more B's you have, especially if you have 5 or more,
the more you and your partner share the task (and joy)
of maintaining closeness in your relationship. It turns
out that partners can feel unhappy if they are the ones
who do more, but also if they are the ones who do less
when it comes to emotional issues.

However, if you had more A's and/or C's and not too many B's, this does not necessarily mean that you have a bad relationship; it simply means that one or the other of you is the leader in various items. You may want to ask yourself how satisfied you are with the way you and your partner express yourselves or experience the items listed on the table.

This is an excellent test to have your partner take as well—and see if you and your partner agree about who does more. Researchers have learned that both partners in a relationship tend to overestimate their own effort in the relationship—whether it has to do with emotions or with housework—and underestimate the effort of their partner. By the way, men tend to overestimate more than women, but both men and women do overestimate.

FAMILY FINANCES INVENTORY

esearch on couples' discord consistently indicates that money is one of the top three areas of conflict in marriage and committed long-term relationships, so it is worthwhile to make sure you and your partner are okay in this area. This test is for couples who share a household. If you aren't sharing a household now, use this quiz to think about how you and the person you are dating deal with money matters; or think about past relationships and how the financial issues were handled.

Directions: Below is a list of common household expenses, with two columns listed for your responses. In the first column, use the scale given below to indicate whose income (from any source) pays for the expenses—yours or your partner's.

Family Finances Scale

1	2	3	4	5	6	7	8	9

mine   both contribute   partner

completely   equally   completely

In the second column, choose from the following scale to indicate how fair you think the financial arrangement is.

Fairness Scale

1	2	3	4	5

very fair   fair   somewhat   unfair   very

fair   unfair

Expenses	Who pays?	Is this fair?	If it is unfair, why is it unfair? *
1. Rent or house payment			
2. Utilities			
3. Groceries			
4. My clothes			
5. Expenses for the children			

Expenses	Who pays?	Is this fair?	If it is unfair, why is it unfair? *
6. Alimony or child-support payments to a previous partner			
7. House cleaning help			
8. Major household appliances			
9. Entertainment or food when out for the evening			
10. My personal spending money (money spent just on myself, not for household expenses)			
11. Major trips and vacations			
12. Gifts			
13. Investments			
Total Scores			

Expenses	Who pays?	Is this fair?	If it is unfair, why is it unfair? *
Number of Questions Answered			
Average Score (divide by number of questions you responded to)			

*This is an open-ended question that does not involve scoring.

Scoring and Evaluation

1. Add up your responses in the first column to obtain your total.
2. Divide total in the first column by the *number of questions* to which you responded (not all were relevant to all people). This is your average score, and it should be between 1 and 9.
3. You can locate the extent to which you share expenses by looking at the Family Finances Scale in the instructions above. Being at one end of the scale or the other (say a 1 or 2 or an 8 or 9) is not necessarily better or worse than being closer to the middle of the scale. What is more important is the extent to which you think the financial arrangements are fair.
4. Add up the total of your responses in the second column. If your average fairness score in the second column is higher than 3, you may want to think about how you can change your financial arrangement to be

more in line with what you (and your partner) are comfortable with.

Answering the question in the third column, "If it is unfair, why is it unfair?" may help you begin to think about if or how this situation could be changed. You may consider whether you or your partner feels that paying for more things entitles either of you to different rights or power in the relationship.

Based on Philip Blumstein and Pepper Schwartz, *American Couples: Money, Work, and Sex,* 1983. Revised by Virginia Rutter and Pepper Schwartz, 1997.

EXTENDED FAMILY COMPATIBILITY TEST

Family obligations tend to be a mixed bag in the lives of couples. Couples benefit from social support, especially from their parents. But parents or other extended-family members can also be a source of conflict. The conflict can arise from what they do or say, such as criticizing you, your partner, or your children—or the conflict can come from issues related to family matters about which you and your partner disagree.

Directions: For each of the 11 statements that follow, indicate the extent to which you agree or disagree by circling the number in the appropriate column.

Statement about adult children, their parents or other extended-family members	Strongly agree	Agree	Neutral	Disagree	Strongly disagree
1. Adult children have an obligation to keep in contact with their parents.	5	4	3	2	1
2. Couples have just as much responsibility to keep in contact with their partner's parents as with their own.*	1	5	4	3	2
3. Couples should not be expected to visit their partner's relatives if they do not want to.*	1	2	3	4	5
4. Except for emergencies, adult children should not take financial assistance or loans from their parents.	1	2	3	4	5
5. It is the responsibility of adult children to be with their parents in times of serious illness even if the adult children have moved some distance from the parents.	5	4	3	2	1

Statement about adult children, their parents or other extended-family members	Strongly agree	Agree	Neutral	Disagree	Strongly disagree
6. If a person's parent has a medical bill and cannot pay, the person is morally obligated to pay the debt.	5	4	3	2	1
7. Couples ought to take turns spending holidays with each other's families.*	5	4	3	2	1
8. When my partner's parents telephone, I typically chat with them at length, especially if my partner isn't around.*	5	4	3	2	1
9. When my parents telephone, my partner chats with them at length, especially if I am not around.	5	4	3	2	1

Statement about adult children, their parents or other extended-family members	Strongly agree	Agree	Neutral	Disagree	Strongly disagree
10. I see or speak to my parents. . .	several times a week [5]	several times a month [4]	several times a year [3]	once per year [2]	less than once per year [1]
*11. I see or speak to my partner's parents. . .	several times a week [5]	several times a month [4]	several times a year [3]	once per year [2]	less than once per year [1]

Total (range: 11–55): _____

Scoring and Evaluation

Add together your responses to these questions. In general the higher your score, the higher your sense of obligation and commitment to family—including your parents and your partner's parents. The ranges listed below are guidelines for interpreting your scores.

• 44–55: Family is at the center of your life and your values.

• 33–43: Family is a high priority.

• 22–32: You are rather cool toward family.

• Below 22: Family isn't at all important.

There are two other ways in which this test can be useful. The first is to ask your partner to take the test, too, and compare answers. How do you differ on the value of family? Several of the issues raised in this questionnaire, such as what to do in times of emergency, often arise with no warning, and forethought (prompted by this test) can help prepare you. Or, you can use this questionnaire as an opportunity to determine the positions you and your partner hold regarding issues such as the emotional and material support for aging parents.

The second use of this inventory relates to attitudes about each other's parents. To learn where you stand, calculate your score for the questions that are marked with an asterisk (*). This total indicates how important your partner's parents are to you. (The range is from 5 to 25.) The higher the score, the greater your commitment to your partner's parents. Now, add up the scores for the other six questions. (The range is from 6 to 30.) The higher this score, the greater your commitment to your own parents.

1. Total of the five "partner's parents family value" questions (*) :   _____
       Average (divide above figure by 5):   _____
2. Total of the six "my parents family value" questions: _____
       Average (divide above figure by 6):   _____

If you want to compare your standards for your family with your standards for your partner's family, divide the first sum by five, and the second sum by six (as indicated above). Chances are your family priority for your parents will be higher than for your partner's parents—this is normal. The question is how large is the discrepancy? The discrepancy may make sense if, for example, one set of parents lives very far away, or for some well-known reason parents are alienated from you and your partner. Comparing these scores, however, can give you a sense of how you balance family obligations between your parents and his/her parents.

There are many other family obligations couples must take into account, including aunts, uncles, siblings, cousins, family friends, and increasingly, stepchildren, former spouses and partners, former stepchildren, and a host of diverse family relationships. For now, you might want to use this opportunity to consider how the two of you balance your obligations to others in your family.

Based on Philip Blumstein and Pepper Schwartz, *American Couples: Money, Work, and Sex,* 1983. Revisions by Virginia Rutter and Pepper Schwartz 1997.

SILENCING THE
SELF SCALE

Psychologist Dana Crowley Jack, who studies why women in relationships are so much more vulnerable to depression than men in relationships, designed this test to measure self-sacrifice that can be a problem for men as well as women.

Women and men tend to self-silence and self-sacrifice for different reasons. Researchers have observed that women in unhappy relationships are more likely to be depressed than men in unhappy relationships because, so the research suggests, women base their self-esteem on the success of intimate relationships more than men do. Often this depression is associated with "silencing the self."

Indeed, our own research has shown a strong connection between marital satisfaction and depression for women (more so than men); in our research this association has also been partly explained by the economic dependence that sometimes accompanies marriage and close relationships for women involved with men.

Directions: Please use the scale below to indicate how much you agree with items on the following questionnaire.

5	4	3	2	1
strongly agree	agree	neutral	disagree	strongly disagree

Statements　　　　　　　　　　　　　　　　　**Response**

1. I think it is best to put myself first because no one else will look out for me. _____

2. I don't speak my feelings in an intimate relationship when I know they will cause disagreement. _____

3. Caring means putting the other person's needs in front of my own. _____

4. Considering my needs to be as important as those of the people I love is selfish. _____

5. I find it is harder to be myself when I am in a close relationship than when I am on my own. _____

6. I tend to judge myself by how I think other people see me. _____

7. I feel dissatisfied with myself because I should be able to do all the things people are supposed to be able to do these days. _____

8. When my partner's needs and feelings conflict with mine, I always state mine clearly. _____

9. In a close relationship my responsibility is to make the other person happy. _____

10. Caring means choosing to do what the other person wants even when I want to do something different. _____

11. In order to feel good about myself I need to feel independent and self-sufficient. _____

12. One of the worst things I can do is be selfish. _____

13. I feel I have to act a certain way to please my partner. _____

14. Instead of risking confrontations in close relationships, I would rather not rock the boat. _____

15. I speak my feelings with my partner, even when it leads to problems or disagreements. _____

16. Often I look happy enough on the outside, but inwardly I feel angry and rebellious. _____

17. In order for my partner to love me, I cannot reveal certain things about myself to him/her. _____

18. When my partner's needs or opinions conflict with mine, rather than asserting my own point of view I usually end up agreeing with him/her. _____

19. When I am in a close relationship I love my sense of who I am. _____

20. When it looks as though certain of my needs can't be met in a relationship, I usually realize that they weren't very important anyway.

21. My partner loves and appreciates me for who I am. _____

22. Doing things just for myself is selfish. _____

23. When I make decisions, other people's thoughts and opinions influence me more than my own thoughts and opinions. _____

24. I rarely express my anger at those close to me. _____

25. I feel that my partner does not know my real self. _____

26. I think it's better to keep my feelings to myself when they do conflict with my partner's. _____

27. I often feel responsible for other people's feelings. _____

28. I find it hard to know what I think and feel because I spend a lot of time thinking about how other people are feeling. _____

29. In a close relationship I don't usually care what we do, as long as the other person is happy. _____

30. I try to bury my feelings when I think they will cause trouble in my close relationship(s). _____

31. I never seem to measure up to my standards
for myself.*   _____

Silencing the Self Score [range: 31–155]:   _____

Scoring and Evaluation

Before adding, reverse score items 1, 8, 11, 15, and 21. To
"reverse score" these items, simply subtract your
response from 6. (If you responded 2, for example,
then your answer is 6 minus 2, or 4.) This means 1
becomes 5; 2 becomes 4; 3 remains the same; 4
becomes 2 and 5 becomes 1. After reverse scoring, add
together all your responses for your silencing the self
score.

Higher scores indicate a higher level of *silencing the self*.
More specifically, this test measures the extent to which
you hide aspects of yourself in your relationship, and
how much you sacrifice yourself for others.

If you scored between 90 and 120, then you tend to put
your partner before yourself, even when it may cause
you difficulty or sadness.

If you scored above 90 on this test, you might try to
voice your own feelings and desires more clearly in
your relationship. This is no easy job; women often
have years of training in self-sacrifice for others to
overcome. But it is an important job for staying
healthy and happy.

If you scored above 120 on this test, then you are probably
submitting to your partner's needs, wishes, and well-

being, and it may be leading to feelings of sadness and even difficult times in your relationship.

*If you answered question 31 with a 4 or 5, list up to three of the standards to which you feel you don't measure up:

_____

_____

_____

[This is not scored.]

Sex-Role Traditionalism and Romanticism Scale

What do sex-role traditionalism and romanticism have to do with each other? Take this test and find out how they relate to each other in different ways for men and for women.

Directions: Using the scale below, indicate how much you personally agree or disagree with each of the following statements in each of the two parts of this test.

1	2	3	4	5	6
strongly disagree	disagree	mildly disagree	mildy agree	agree	strongly agree

SEX-ROLE TRADITIONALISM

1. One of the most important things a mother can do for her daughter is to prepare her for being a wife. _____

2. When a couple is going somewhere by car, it's better for the man to do most of the driving. _____

3. If husband and wife both have full-time jobs, the husband should devote just as much time to house-keeping as the wife should. _____ _____

4. The women's liberation movement exaggerates the problems faced by women in America today. _____

5. In marriage, the husband should take the lead in decision-making. _____

6. It's reasonable that the wife should have major responsibility for care of the children. _____

7. It's just as appropriate for a woman to hold a door open for a man as vice versa. _____ _____

8. Working women should not be expected to sacrifice their careers for the sake of home duties to any greater extent than men. _____ _____

9. Women could run most businesses as well as men could. _____ _____

10. If both husband and wife work full-time, her career should be just as important as his in determining where the family lives.   _____   _____

Total Sex-Role Traditionalism Score (see reverse scoring instructions before completing):   _____

ROMANTICISM

11. Lovers ought to expect a certain amount of disillusionment after marriage.   _____   _____
12. To be truly in love is to be in love forever.   _____
13. As long as they at least love each other, two people should have no trouble getting along together in marriage.   _____
14. A person should marry whomever s/he loves regardless of social position.   _____
15. One should not marry against the serious advice of one's parents.   _____   _____
16. Most of us could sincerely love any one of several people equally well.   _____   _____

Total Romanticism Score (see reverse scoring instructions before completing):   _____

Scoring and Evaluation

Before you add your responses together, questions 3, 7, 8, 9, 10, 11, 15, and 16 (those questions followed by two scoring spaces) should be "reverse scored." To reverse-score these items, subtract your responses from 7. So, for example if you answered number 3 with a "5," your reverse scored answer would be 7 minus 5, or 2. A second scoring space is provided for each question where reverse scoring is required. After you have reversed-scored those items mentioned above, add up your respective scores in the Sex-Role Traditionalism and Romanticism parts.

Sex-Role Traditionalism Subscore

Higher scores (in the range of 1 through 60) indicate higher levels of traditional sex-role beliefs. Traditional sex-role beliefs center on the idea of men being dominant in heterosexual relationships. Nontraditional sex role beliefs, also called egalitarian beliefs, center on the idea that men's and women's roles in heterosexual relationships are flexible and, for the most part, interchangeable.

- Traditionals tend to have scores between 40 and 60.
- Moderates tend to have scores between 20 and 40.
- Egalitarians tend to have scores between 1 and 20.

There is an interesting gender difference on this part of the test: in research on college students using this questionnaire, men who were "egalitarians" were nearly as likely as men who were "traditionals" to expect to get married (over 90%). For women, however, there were differences. Traditional and moderate women all expected to marry, while fewer than 90% of egalitarian women expected to marry. This suggests that if you are a woman interested in egalitarianism, you may want to be particularly careful in looking for a partner who shares your values.

Romanticism Subscore

Higher scores (in the range between 1 and 36) indicate higher levels of romanticism. Romanticism in this case means the extent to which you believe in the power and importance of "one true love." Scores above 24 are *highly romantic.*

The romanticism test has been used with the sex-role traditionalism questionnaire in research because of the interesting relationship between romanticism and sex roles. Men who are "traditional" when it comes to sex roles tend to be high on romanticism, also. The same association of traditionality and romanticism, however, does not exist, typically, for women. Another way to think of this is that women, more so than men, can experience egalitarian relationships as romantic.

If you believe in egalitarian relationships, a man's high romanticism score might help flag his sex-role traditionalism. This might make you wary, but it shouldn't rule him out unless you have other information.

SOME SERIOUS RELATIONSHIP ISSUES

IN THIS SECTION YOU WILL LEARN: WHETHER YOUR BEHAVIORS TOWARD EACH OTHER ARE LEADING TO PROBLEMS • WHETHER YOU ARE EXPERIENCING ANY OF THE MOST COMMON RELATIONSHIP-THREATENING PROBLEMS • WHAT ALTERNATIVES TO THE RELATIONSHIP YOU PERCEIVE • IF YOU MIGHT BE IN AN EMOTIONALLY OR PHYSICALLY ABUSIVE RELATIONSHIP • WHETHER YOUR RELATIONSHIP IS INCHING TOWARD ITS DEMISE

PREDICT QUIZ

The "Predict Quiz" is based on research that followed couples from courtship long into their married (and in some cases, divorced) years. The researchers on this study and others who do similar work learn about couples' relationships by asking them questions, having them respond to questionnaires, and observing couples as they interact in conflict and in confrontational situations. They even hook couples up to physiological monitors to see how fast their hearts beat at different times, which adds new insight into couples' conflict.

This questionnaire taps the issues that are most useful for researchers and therapists to predict divorce or breakup. Professional counselors also use these questions to help guide them in their interventions with couples, and you can use this questionnaire to help you focus on what is happening in your relationship.

Before you take this test, you may wish to recall a recent conversation during which you and your partner talked about a disappointment, an annoyance, a problem, or a gripe. Then read the statements listed below and determine whether the statement is true—or mostly true— or false—or mostly false—as a description of the way you react typically during discussions about problems.

Relationship Behaviors	True or False?
1. I sometimes nag at my partner in order to get him/her to talk.	T F
2. It is very easy for me to get angry with my partner.	T F
3. My partner does not try very hard to understand me.	T F
4. When my partner does something that makes me angry, I usually let him/her know about it.	T F
5. I often push my partner to talk about issues even when it is clear that my partner doesn't want to talk.	T F
6. I feel good after getting angry.	T F
Subscore 1 (number of "True" responses to 1–6):	_____

Relationship Behaviors	True or False?
7. If I had my choice I'd avoid conflicts and disagreements.	T F
8. When my partner brings up a relationship issue, I tend to withdraw, become silent, or refuse to discuss the matter further.	T F
9. I often find myself saying, "I don't care. Whatever you want is fine with me" when I am asked for an opinion.	T F
10. I often agree with my partner's wishes just to end a discussion.	T F
11. Sometimes I don't talk to my partner because I've noticed that talking leads to fighting.	T F
12. I often sit and stare at my partner, not saying anything.	T F
Subscore 2 (number of "True" responses to 7–12):	_____
13. During problem discussions, my stomach often feels as if it's all tied up in knots.	T F
14. I often feel a lump in my throat when I argue with my partner.	T F
15. My body often becomes tense during a relationship problem discussion.	T F

Relationship Behaviors	True or False?
16. My heart often speeds up or races during our conversation.	T F
17. I often feel very anxious at the start of a problem discussion.	T F
18. I would describe myself as very emotionally charged or tense whenever there is a major disagreement.	T F
Subscore 3 (number of "True" responses to 13–18):	_____
19. I am basically unhappy with my relationship.	T F
20. I have often felt like leaving my partner.	T F
21. I often don't feel close to my partner.	T F
22. We hardly ever do any fun things together.	T F
23. I'm not sure I really love my partner anymore.	T F
24. I am not satisfied with our sex life.	T F
25. I often do not feel supported by my partner.	T F
Subscore 4 (number of "True" responses to 19–25):	_____

Relationship Behaviors	True or False?
26. At the beginning of most conversations about typical relationship problems, I believe that we will not be able to get close to a satisfying resolution.	T F
27. I have little confidence in being able to discuss a significant relationship problem with my partner without fighting.	T F
28. In five out of ten disagreements with my partner I will be unable to make any headway in reaching a happy solution.	T F
Subscore 5 (number of "True" responses to 26–28):	_____

Total Number of "True" Responses: _____

Scoring and Evaluation

Add the number of true responses for the whole test and for each subscore.

If you answered mostly false on this test, then you are doing well.

Subscore 1: If you answered true to four or more in this subscore, then you are a *pursuer*. You are in the role of seeking contact with your partner.

Subscore 2: If you answered true to four or more in this section, then you are a *distancer*. Your response to conflict is to avoid it. (You will recall that in section 3, demand/withdraw patterns were discussed in the Communication Patterns Questionnaire. Here they are discussed in the context of behavior as well as communication.)

Subscore 3: If you responded true to four or more in this section then you are a *physiological responder*. When conflict arises, your body shifts to prepare itself for a fight—even if you are not engaging in a fight. The problem with becoming aroused during discussions is that it makes it more difficult to think clearly. If you find yourself getting aroused—heart racing, palms sweating, face flushed—then you should take time out to calm down for at least twenty minutes before returning to address the problem at hand.

Subscore 4: This is a measure of your current *unhappiness*. If you responded true to four or more of these questions, then your relationship may be in a lot of trouble. Should you stay? Can you stay? How can you stay? What can you do? There are resources listed in the back of this book you could explore using; and you can also start by talking to a friend or a family member, if you can.

Subscore 5: This is a measure of your current *expectations*. Even if you have only one true answer in this set, it is a sign that you are giving up on your relationship, and that along with being unhappy now with your relationship, you actually don't expect things to get better in the future. You've lost hope. Now is the time to think about what you are going to do about it.

If you scored high in three out of five of the subscales involved, then you might want to pay special attention to various aspects of your relationship. And a good place to start, as you can guess from the questionnaire above, is how you handle conflict with your partner.

Cliff Notarius, Ph.D., and Howard Markman, Ph.D., who designed this quiz, have developed courses for couples to take at the beginning of their relationship to help them avoid getting into trouble areas in the first place—as well as for couples who need or want help improving their communication and behavior toward each other. A referral source for such couples' courses is in the resources section at the end of this book.

Reprinted by permission of The Putnam Publishing Group from *We Can Work It Out* by Clifford Notarius and Howard Markman. Copyright © 1993 Clifford Notarius and Howard Markman.

MARITAL AGENDAS PROTOCOL

This questionnaire is used to help you identify the areas in your relationship where you have problems or disagreements. The designers of this questionnaire used their research to determine the most common sources of conflict in couples. Those problems are the ones listed on the questionnaire. These questions could help you understand problem areas that you have with your mate.

Directions: Please read each of the following questions carefully and note your responses in the spaces provided. Please answer all questions and leave no answers blank. If you add examples (under "other") for one question please add the same examples to the rest of the questions in the section.

PART 1A: SERIOUS PROBLEMS TO ME

Consider the list of issues that all relationships must face, on the following page. In the first column, rate how much of a problem each area is currently in your relationship with a number from 0 (not at all a problem) to 100 (a severe problem). For example, if money is no problem, you might enter a 0; if somewhat of a problem, you might enter a 25; a severe problem, you might enter a 100. Be sure to *rate all areas* by entering a number between 0 and 100 next to each relationship issue.

PART 1B: SERIOUS PROBLEMS TO MY PARTNER

In the second column, predict how you partner will respond to the same topics.

Marital Agenda Protocol Scale:

0 100
not at all a   a severe and serious
   problem   problem

	1A	1B
Money	_____	_____
Communication	_____	_____
Family	_____	_____
Children	_____	_____
Sex	_____	_____
Religion	_____	_____
Recreation	_____	_____
Friends	_____	_____
Alchohol & Drugs	_____	_____
Health	_____	_____
Jealousy	_____	_____
Work or careers	_____	_____
Other		
(_____)	_____	_____
(_____)	_____	_____

PART 2: RATE OF RESOLVED CONFLICT

Imagine the next ten disagreements you and your partner will have in each of the following areas. Indicate how many of these ten disagreements in each area you do believe you and your partner will resolve to your mutual satisfaction. In answering this question, rate each item on a scale of 0 to 10 whereby "0" means "My partner and I will not resolve *any* disagreement on this topic." A "4" means you believe "My partner and I will resolve 4 out of 10 disagreements on this topic," and a "10" means "My partner and I *will resolve all* disagreements on this topic."

Money	_____	Work or	
Communication	_____	Careers	_____
Family	_____	Household	
Children	_____	Tasks	_____
Sex	_____	Other	
Religion	_____	(_____)	_____
Recreation	_____	Other	
Friends	_____	(_____)	_____
Alcohol/Drugs	_____	Other	
Health	_____	(_____)	_____
Jealousy	_____		

PART 3: RESPONSIBILITY AND FAULT

Who do you believe is responsible for unresolved disagreements in each of the relationship areas on the list? For each area check the box under "me" if you believe that you are primarily responsible for unresolved disagreements. Check the box under "partner" if you believe your partner is primarily responsible. Check the box under "both" if you believe you and your partner are equally responsible for unresolved disagreements. Check the box under "neither" if you believe that neither you nor your partner is responsible for unresolved disagreements. Again, if you added any areas to the list, please enter these in the spaces provided and rate them also. If you have no unresolved disagreements in the area, check "always agree."

Who is responsible for unresolved disagreements? Check one.

Issue	me	part-ner	both	neither	always agree
Money	☐	☐	☐	☐	☐
Communi-cation	☐	☐	☐	☐	☐
Family	☐	☐	☐	☐	☐
Children	☐	☐	☐	☐	☐
Sex	☐	☐	☐	☐	☐
Religion	☐	☐	☐	☐	☐
Recreation	☐	☐	☐	☐	☐
Friends	☐	☐	☐	☐	☐
Alcohol & Drugs	☐	☐	☐	☐	☐
Health	☐	☐	☐	☐	☐
Jealousy	☐	☐	☐	☐	☐
Work or Careers	☐	☐	☐	☐	☐
Household Tasks	☐	☐	☐	☐	☐
Other (_____)	☐	☐	☐	☐	☐
Other (_____)	☐	☐	☐	☐	☐
Other (_____)	☐	☐	☐	☐	☐

Scoring and Evaluation

We developed the following questions to help you understand the results of the three parts of this questionnaire.

Part 1A "Serious Problems": How many areas were rated above 50? The more problem areas, the more areas you have where you can focus to improve your relationship.

List problems rated above 50:

_____   _____   _____   _____   _____

_____   _____   _____   _____   _____

_____   _____   _____   _____

Part 1B: How many areas were rated above 50? Note in particular in which areas you think that you and your partner don't agree. These are probably the areas in Part 2 where you don' t resolve your fights effectively. Problems I rated above 50 for my partner:

_____   _____   _____   _____   _____

_____   _____   _____   _____   _____

_____   _____   _____   _____

Part 2 "Rate of Resolved Conflict": Reviewing your responses to Part 2 is especially important. Couples have a variety of successful styles of interaction. One of them, for example, an "argumentative style," may describe a couple which is basically happy and although they have many conflicts, they also know how to resolve them. Thus, you may have reported that you and your partner have a lot of disagreements but if you know how to resolve your disagreements, fighting itself isn't a problem. If you don't know how to reach a resolution, this is when fighting and disagreements contribute to the deterioration of a relationship.

List problems in Part 2 with a score of 4 or lower:

_____ _____ _____ _____ _____

_____ _____ _____ _____ _____

_____ _____ _____ _____ _____

Part 3 "Responsibility and Fault": How many times do you blame yourself?

How many times do you blame your partner?

Do you take an "I'm good and you're bad" position in your relationship (i.e., blame your partner often)? Or do you take an "I'm bad and you're good" position (i.e., blame yourself often)? Does your partner do this, too? If you find that you and your partner are exchanging blame, think about why you are blaming each other. Is there any way to reduce the level of blaming?

The Marital Agendas Protocol was developed by Clifford I. Notarius and Nelly Z. Vanzetti at the Center for Family Psychology, Catholic University of America, Washington, D.C. Dr. Notarius maintains a clinical practice in Washington, D.C., and Dr. Vanzetti in Tulsa, Oklahoma. Notarius is coauthor of *We Can Work It Out* (Putnam, 1993). Reprinted by permission of authors.

ALTERNATIVES
SCALE

Thinking about alternatives to a current relationship doesn't seem like a very loving thing to do but, taken in conjunction with other tests in this book, the Alternatives Scale may clarify how you feel about the future of your relationship. However, this test does not and cannot predict whether you and your partner are in fact on your way to a breakup.

Directions: How likely do you imagine each of the following would be? Decide whether you think each item would be impossible, possible, probable, or certain—and check the appropriate box.

How likely is it that:	Impossible	Possible, but not likely	Probable	Certain
1. You could get another, better partner?	1	2	3	4
2. You could get another partner as good as this partner?	1	2	3	4
3. You would be able to live as well as you do now?	1	2	3	4
4. You could continue to maintain your standard of living?	1	2	3	4
5. You could be quite satisfied without a relationship?	1	2	3	4
6. You would be sad, but get over it quickly?	1	2	3	4
7. Your prospects for a happy future would be bleak?	4	3	2	1
8. Your life would be ruined?	4	3	2	1

Total [range: 8–32]: _____

Scoring and Evaluation

Add up your answers to obtain your Alternatives score. The lower your score, the worse you *think* your alternatives to your current relationship are. Based on our evaluation of the research, if your score is 13 to 16, your alternatives don't seem bright to you. If your score is 12 or lower, you see no alternatives at all.

It turns out that these scores mean different things depending upon whether partners score in the satisfied or happy range on other tests. So, for example, if you scored in the troubled range on the Predict Quiz at the beginning of this section, and now you have scored 16 or lower on the Alternatives Scale, then this test indicates that you feel trapped in your relationship. You can't imagine a better situation, even though your current situation does not seem all that wonderful. People in troubled relationships who score high on the Alternatives Scale—above 18—might be on their way out of the relationship.

However, if you scored in the happy range on the Predict Questionnaire, or if you scored high on the Relationship Assessment Scale in Section Two of the book, then a therapist might interpret a low score on the Alternatives Questionnaire as another sign of happiness and commitment. If you are high on love and commitment, and you also scored above 18 on the Alternatives Scale, then you have the benefit of being in love and feeling a lot of self-confidence and independence regarding your well-being.

Reported in "Marital Alternatives and Marital Disruption," *Journal of Marriage and the Family* 43 (1981): pp. 889–97, by University of North Carolina sociologist Richard Udry. Copyright © 1981 by the National Council on Family Relations, 3989 Central Ave. N.E., #550, Minneapolis, MN 55421. Reprinted by permission of NCFR and the author. Scoring interpretations based in part on our unpublished data analysis using the National Survey of Families and Households I.

CONFLICT TACTICS SCALE

No matter how well a couple gets along, there are times when they disagree on major discussions, get annoyed about something the other person does, or just have spats or fights because they're in a bad mood, tired, or for some other reason. They also use many different ways of trying to settle their differences. This test evaluates the tactics you and your partner use.

Directions: This test has two parts. In the first part, review the list of tactics and indicate whether your partner has engaged in any of these ways of dealing with conflict in the past year. In the second part, you will do the same with respect to yourself. Score according to the following scale:

0	1	2	3	4	5	6
Never	Once	Twice	3–5 Times	6–10 Times	11–20 Times	More Than 20 Times

PART 1: THE THINGS MY PARTNER HAS DONE IN FIGHTS WITH ME

Conflict Tactics
Section One: Constructive Tactics

Discussed an issue calmly. _____

Got information to back up his/her side of
things. _____

Brought in or tried to bring in someone to
help settle things. _____

Subscore (sum of Section One): _____

Section Two: Destructive Tactics

Insulted or swore at me. _____

Stomped out of the room, the house, or the
yard. _____

Cried. _____

Did or said something to spite me. _____

Threatened to hit or throw something at me. _____

Threw or smashed or hit or kicked something. _____

Threw something at me. _____

Pushed, grabbed, or shoved me.   _____

Slapped me.   _____

Kicked, bit, or hit with a fist.   _____

Hit or tried to hit with something.   _____

Beat me up.   _____

Threatened with a knife or gun.   _____

Used a knife or gun.   _____

Subscore (sum of Section Two):   _____

PART 2: THE THINGS I HAVE DONE IN FIGHTS WITH MY PARTNER

Conflict Tactics
Section One: Constructive Tactic

Discussed an issue calmly.   _____

Got information to back up my side of things.   _____

Brought in or tried to bring in someone to
    help settle things.   _____

Subscore (sum of Section One):   _____

Section Two: Destructive Tactic

Insulted or swore at my partner.   _____

Stomped out of the room, the house, or the
    yard.   _____

Cried.   _____

Did or said something to spite my partner.   _____

Threatened to hit or throw something at my
partner.   ————

Threw or smashed or hit or kicked something.   ————

Threw something at my partner.   ————

Pushed, grabbed, or shoved my partner.   ————

Slapped my partner.   ————

Kicked, bit, or hit with a fist.   ————

Hit or tried to hit with something.   ————

Beat up my partner.   ————

Threatened with a knife or gun.   ————

Used a knife or gun.   ————

Subscore (sum of Section Two):   ————

Scoring and Evaluation:

Add up your responses and record them on the table on
the following page. In the first row (marked Section
One), you should record your scores from Part 1, Section One and for Part 2, Section One. In the second
row (marked Section Two) you should record your
scores from Part 1, Section Two and from Part 2, Section Two.

CONFLICT TACTICS SCORES

	Part 1 (Partner's Scores)	Part 2 (My Scores)	Range	Interpretation
Section One (Constructive tactics)			0-18	Higher scores (above 8) indicate constructive conflict tactics
Section Two (Destructive tactics)			0-84	Higher scores indicate destructive conflict tactics. Even one destructive episode, however, can be abuse. Read below to think about the function of any violence or aggression in your relationship.

If your Section One scores for you or your partner are high, this indicates that you and your partner engage in constructive, safe ways of dealing with conflict. You may experience a lot or a little conflict; you may be very happy together, or not so happy together, but if you engage in calm debate over the issues, you are being safe and respectful of the well-being of your partner.

Section Two of the Conflict Tactics Scale focuses in great detail on destructive conflict tactics that couples experience. As the scoring interpretation indicates, even a little destructive tactics can be a big problem. Couples therapists indicate that about 75 percent of their clients have experienced some physical aggression. In addition, domestic violence research indicates that as many as one-third of all wives are subject to physical aggression and abuse by their partners at some point during the marriage. Sometimes partners don't even know that the acts listed in Section Two constitute aggression and abuse that are, or can be, indicative of a dangerous, depressing, or destructive relationship.

One of the things that the Conflict Tactics Scale does *not* measure is the *function* of aggression in couples. What do we mean by the function of physical aggression? Acts of physical aggression have different meanings depending upon whether they have the effect of *controlling* a partner's behavior. Although women may respond to physical aggression with physical aggression themselves, the research indicates that women tend not to be the initiators of violence, and that any aggression on women's part does not function as a way to gain power and control over the other person.

Because every situation is different, it is quite difficult to create a questionnaire to determine what purpose aggression serves in relationships. Therapists and researchers are

more likely to be helpful when they observe couples argu-
ing and interview them in detail to learn about the function of any violence. This is a very difficult and serious
topic but one that needed to be addressed in this book.

Several questions about aggression in your relationship
help to evaluate whether it's abuse: If you are afraid or
have ever been injured by your partner, this, according to
the experts, is abuse. What constitutes injury? Some
researchers put it this way: If you wake up the next morning (after a physical altercation) and you're not yourself,
you've been injured. Resources referred to at the end of
this book may be of interest to you if this questionnaire
raised concerns about your relationship.

The Conflict Tactics Scale was created by Professor Murray Straus,
Ph.D., Director of the Family Research Laboratory at the University of
New Hampshire.

MARITAL INSTABILITY SCALE

One of the benefits of this test is to help you recognize the thoughts and behaviors that sometimes are associated with marital instability—whether or not your relationship will stand the test of time. Every relationship is different, however, and every relationship has different thresholds for "instability."

Directions: After each of the statements about thoughts and behaviors, mark the most accurate answer from: Has never occurred; has occurred; has occurred in the past three years; occurs now.

Statement	Never	Ever	In Last 3 Years	Now
1. I have thought my marriage is in trouble.	0	1	2	3
2. I have talked to others about marital problems.	0	1	2	3
3. I have talked to friends about marital problems.	0	1	2	3
4. Spouse has talked to others about marital problems.	0	1	2	3
5. Spouse has thought our marriage is in trouble.	0	1	2	3
6. I have thought about divorce.	0	1	2	3
7. Spouse has thought about divorce.	0	1	2	3
8. Either spouse or I has seriously suggested divorce.	0	1	2	3
9. I favor divorce.	0	1	2	3
10. My spouse favors divorce.	0	1	2	3
11. I have initiated conversation about divorce.	0	1	2	3

Statement	Never	Ever	In Last 3 Years	Now
12. I favor divorce more than spouse.	0	1	2	3
13. I have discussed consulting or have consulted with an attorney.	0	1	2	3
14. I have discussed division of property.	0	1	2	3
15. I have discussed problems of living apart.	0	1	2	3
16. I have discussed filing or actually filed a petition.	0	1	2	3
17. I have discussed divorce with family member who approves.	0	1	2	3
18. I have discussed divorce with friend who approves.	0	1	2	3
19. I have experienced separation.	0	1	2	3

Total (sum of responses) [range: 0-57]: _____

Scoring and Evaluation

Relationship stability—or instability—refers to whether a relationship can stand the test of time. In research by sociologists and psychologists, higher scores on this test were associated with greater likelihood of breaking up. This test cannot tell you whether you are going to get a divorce or not but the higher your score, the more your marriage shares characteristics with marriages that may be at higher risk for ending.

From "Measuring Marital Instability" by Alan Booth (Pennsylvania State University), David Johnson, John N. Edwards, *Journal of Marriage and the Family* 45 (1983): 387-393. Reprinted by permission of the author and the National Council on Family Relations. Copyright © 1983 by the National Council on Family Relations, 3989 Central Ave. NE, #550, Minneapolis, MN 55421.

WHAT NOW? ADDITIONAL RESOURCES FOR YOU

BOOKS

If you want to learn more about the topics raised in this book, we recommend the following very useful books by some of the social scientists and therapists whose work is described in this book.

- *When Lovers Make War,* Andrew Christensen and Neil Jacobson (Guilford Press, 1998).
- *When Partners Become Parents: A Big Life Change for Couples,* Carolyn Pape Cowan and Philip Cowan (Basic Books, 1992).
- *Why Marriages Succeed or Fail,* John Gottman (Simon & Schuster, 1994).
- *Love, Sex and Intimacy,* Elaine Hatfield and Richard Rapson (HarperCollins, 1993).
- *Becoming Orgasmic,* Julia Heiman and Joseph LoPiccolo (Simon & Schuster, 1988).

- *Romantic Love,* Susan P. Hendrick and Clyde Hendrick (Sage Books, 1992).
- *Silencing the Self: Women and Depression,* Dana Crowley Jack (Harvard University Press, 1991).
- *When Men Batter Women: New Insights into Ending Abusive Relationships,* Neil Jacobson and John Gottman (Simon & Schuster, 1998).
- *We Can Work It Out,* Cliff Notarius and Howard Markman (Putnam, 1994).
- *The New Kinsey Report,* June Reinisch (St. Martin's Press, 1991).
- *Love Between Equals,* Pepper Schwartz (Free Press, 1994).
- *The Great Sex Weekend,* Pepper Schwartz and Janet Lever, (Putnam, 1998).

COURSES

Courses on couples issues have grown more and more common and are helpful both to couples who are doing well—and couples who are having problems. Below is a national referral source.

The *Coalition for Marriage, Family, and Couples Education.* This organization serves as a clearinghouse for couples education programs. Couples education courses focus on teaching couples skills so they can solve their own problems. The courses are designed to address a variety of aspects of intimate relationships, from improving communication to enhancing emotional connections between partners. To locate a course in your area visit their Web site directory at: www.smartmarriages.com

PSYCHOTHERAPY

If you want help regarding individual or relationship concerns or questions, you may wish to find a therapist or counselor. Below are several national organizations that can help you find a qualified, licensed therapist or counselor.

In addition, you can look for a psychologist or social worker in your yellow pages by looking under either of two headings: psychologist (for Ph.D. and Psy.D.-psychologists who are licensed in your state to practice psychotherapy) or psychotherapist (look for people with an M.S.W. who are certified mental health providers in your state).

When searching for a therapist do not hesitate to ask about his/her training and the kind of treatment s/he provides, to make sure that s/he has had experience dealing with the particular kinds of issues that you or you and your partner are concerned about.

The *National Association of Social Workers* can refer you to certified social workers in your area who specialize in the kinds of issues that you are concerned with. When you call their toll-free line, indicate what kind of expertise you are looking for in a therapist. The toll-free number is 1-800-638-8799.

The *Association for the Advancement of Behavior Therapy* can refer you to some of the over 4,500 psychologists, psychiatrists, physicians, nurses, social workers, and other mental health professionals who use behavior therapy or cognitive therapy to treat many different problems. Behavior therapy and cognitive therapy are research-based forms of treatment that are goal-focused, generally short-term, and often drug free. These therapists usually focus on current situations rather than past ones. You can write or call the AABT central office or visit their Web site in order to receive a list of therapists in your area, a fact sheet regarding the issues you are concerned with, and "Guidelines for Choosing a Behavior Therapist." There is no charge, but AABT requests that you send a $5 check or money order to cover postage and handling costs.

CONTACT:

AABT
305 Seventh Avenue
NY, NY 10001
phone 212-647-1890
fax 212-647-1865
Web site: server.psyc.vt.edu/aabt

The *American Association for Sex Educators, Counselors, and Therapists* can refer you to certified sexuality therapists in your area. Send a self-addressed, stamped, business-size envelope to

American Association for Sex Educators, Counselors, and Therapists (AASECT)
P.O. Box 238
Mount Vernon, Iowa 52314-0238

The *Sexuality Information and Education Council of the United States* (SIECUS) is a national organization that provides information about sexual health. To contact their library, call 212-819-9790.

OTHER ISSUES

Several tests in this book asked questions or raised issues related to abuse in relationships. If you have questions or concerns about these kinds of things in your relationship, or just want to learn more, you can contact the Domestic Violence Hotline at 1-800-562-6052. This is a toll-free call in the United States and Canada. They can provide an information packet and direct you to local support agencies in your area.